AF835084

Paul Bennett is a Solicitor, Mediator and Arbitrator who advises on SRA investigations and regulatory action, Anti-Money Laundering, employment and partnership law in the specialist Professional Practice Team at Aaron & Partners LLP a firm of Solicitors with offices in Manchester, Chester and Shrewsbury.

Paul's work is national and his experience includes advising hundreds of law firms from High Street to City & US Law Firms. In 2008 he was appointed by the Attorney General to the Regional Panel of Counsel as a Solicitor Advocate.

A Law Society of England and Wales Law Management Section Committee member he Chaired the Small Firms Division Committee in 2015 having previously been a Managing Director who sold a successful niche law firm he had started. His next book, A Practical Guide to the SRA Code of Conduct [2018], is due to be published later this year by Law Brief Publishing.

Previously Paul has written occasionally on his areas of practice for the Law Society Gazette, Legal Futures, Modern Law Magazine and the Solicitors Journal. Paul regularly speaks at CPD conferences and webinars.

www.aaronandpartners.com/business/professional-practices/
Email: paul.bennett@aaronandpartners.com
Tel: 01743 453 685

A Practical Guide to Compliance for Personal Injury Firms Working With Claims Management Companies

A Practical Guide to Compliance for Personal Injury Firms Working With Claims Management Companies

Paul Bennett
Solicitor Advocate (All Proceedings)
LLB (Hons) LLM PG Dip
Chartered Manager
Legal and business adviser to Solicitors and Law Firms

Law Brief Publishing

Published 2017 by
Law Brief Publishing
30 The Parks
Minehead
Somerset
TA24 8BT

www.lawbriefpublishing.com

Paperback: 978-1-911035-21-3

This book is dedicated to my ever supportive (and understanding) wife, Sue, and my daughters, Martha & Nancy, who have seen less of me than they should have done during the writing process. Thank you for your love and patience.

ACKNOWLEDGEMENTS

My thanks go to my publishers, Tim and Garry, for allowing my dream of having a book published to be realised. It has been fun working with you and I look forward to the next book!

I am grateful to my colleagues Jo and Natalie for their diligent typing when my fingers got overwhelmed and for the proof reading of the chapters I typed myself.

At the outset of writing this book the SRA were co-operative and kindly confirmed I could use extracts of their published material provided its source was acknowledged and you will note I have utilised extracts from materials and acknowledged the source throughout the work. The full versions are, of course, available on their website for free at https://www.sra.org.uk/home/home.page, so there is no benefit to readers to reproduce fully in a book.

Paul Bennett
August 2017

ABBREVIATIONS

ASA	Advertising Standards Authority
Brexit	The UK's leaving from the European Union
CAP	Committee on Advertising Practice
CMC	Claims Management Company (authorised under the Compensation Act 2006)
CMR	Claims Management Regulator (the Division of the Ministry of Justice who supervise CMCs)
Code of Conduct 2011	The SRA's guide to conduct for solicitors which came into force on 6th October 2011
Code of Conduct [2018]	The SRA's proposed guide to conduct for solicitors which may come into force in 2018
COFA	Compliance Officer for Finance and Administration
COLP	Compliance Officer for Legal Practice
DMA	The Direct Marketing Association
DPA	Data Protection Act 1998
LASPO	Legal Aid, Sentencing and Punishment of Offenders Act 2012
LeO	Legal Ombudsman
PECR	The Privacy and Electronic Communications (EC Directive) Regulations 2003
SRA	Solicitors Regulation Authority

Contents

CHAPTER ONE
INTRODUCTION

Overview

This book has a single ambitious objective: to help personal injury firms survive at the most challenging time in history for many such firms by enabling them to work with Claims Management Companies (CMCs[1]) to secure work which complies with possibly the most demanding compliance regime in legal history.

Since the inception of the Solicitors Regulation Authority (SRA) in January 2007 to separate the regulatory functions of the Law Society of England and Wales (the Law Society) in relation to professional conduct, and importantly, misconduct, the Law Society has been diminished and operates in the spheres of policy, advice functions to law firms and individual solicitors and as a quasi-trade union (known as a representative body). The Solicitors Regulatory Authority (SRA) by contrast has been increasingly assertive on policy and aggressive in its pursuit of consumer (never clients in SRA speak) interests in pursing those Solicitors and firms who take a chance or cut corners.

You need to understand your role, your risks and your obligations to operate in this new environment.

How to use this book?

This book is intended to be used in three ways. Firstly, as an introductory guide to those in the personal injury sector who want to work with CMCs and perhaps are embarking on new contractual relationships with CMCs. Readers who are in a management role, whether within in a personal injury firm in management only or when formally appointed and authorised by the SRA for a role such Compliance Officer for Legal Practice (COLP) or Compliance Officer for Finance and Administration (COFA) may wish to read it from cover to cover to

1 Claims Management Companies are defined by law and in later chapters we will examine what one is and why your firm may wish to work with them.

understand the challenge, the risks and most importantly the opportunities to deliver profitable practice by using compliance as a management tool.

The second use is when you need to dip in and out of the checklists in later chapters for guidance on a specific point. **Each situation is unique and there is general information in this book but not specific legal advice (and if you want to know how it applies to your individual position then please instruct me to guide you).**

Thirdly, for Claims Management Companies who will often need to understand their clients (law firms) needs on compliance to retain work from law firms who are challenged repeatedly by their professional obligations. Key is the message that professional obligations on solicitors come before any commercial wishes. For non-lawyers this may appear madness but it is essential they understand this point because once the SRA investigate a personal injury firm they may otherwise undermine the commercial relationship through their actions (such as a condition on a firm's authorisation).

The structure of the book

Other than terminology each chapter is self-contained. For this reason you will find a list of abbreviations. This is to enable you to dip in and out on a specific issue if you wish.

Each chapter looks at something which can be isolated but with compliance there is always the key question:

- If I do this, what are the full consequences?

This key question is the source of much of my day-to-day workload advising law firms across England and Wales. Points get missed or misunderstood and the SRA, when they visit, challenge what the firm has done and why. A book, as my publishers keep reminding me, is generic and if you wish to know how the legislation, guidance and risks apply to your own situation you will need to instruct me to advise as this book is not legal advice.

If you are looking at an isolated point you need therefore to ask yourself: If I do this, what are the full consequences?

Conclusion

This book is designed to help you stay compliant and to challenge your thinking. It of course is designed to help you but if you are unsure you should take specialist advice as the firms of the future will be those the SRA (or its replacement in due course) will leave alone as they do not appear to be a high risk against their current agenda.

Finally, the law and regulations quoted are as of the 1st August 2017.

CHAPTER TWO
THE CHALLENGE: THE SRA AND THE COMPLIANCE AGENDA

Compliance basics

You may think this is obvious, but every day I advise law firms who have failed to step back and challenge their own way of working. For compliance to be effective you need to take a helicopter view and view it from an external perspective.

In this chapter we will look at the challenges which are known to exist and set some of them out so you can ask yourself when considering the later chapters:

1. What does this mean for my business?

2. How would we demonstrate our compliance?

3. Who is going to take the lead on this compliance project?

4. Why are they the right person?

Like many regulators, the SRA focuses on regulation by risk management, i.e. if something is high risk they are more likely to look at it. The SRA publish their thinking on risk so personal injury firms can assess the risks and then reflect on how they apply in their own businesses.

It is worth bearing in mind at all times that guidance from regulators can change and the Courts can reinterpret legislation at any time. Nothing is certain in this field. Additionally, this book is not legal advice. My publisher wants me to remind you in each Chapter that you should instruct me to give advice on your specific situation if you want it and the factual circumstances your business faces can be assessed and advised on.

SRA OVERVIEW

What do the SRA actually do?

The SRA's remit under the Legal Services Act 2007 (LSA2007) is to regulate in the interests of consumers. The LSA2007 states in Section 1 eight regulatory objectives. The very first of these is "protecting and promoting the public interest".[1]

The SRA state their objectives as:

> *"Our purpose is to protect the public*
>
> - *by ensuring that solicitors meet high standards, and*
> - *By acting when risks are identified."*[2]

In simple terms their role is protect the general public from solicitors' conduct (read misconduct) and to set and enforce standards.

This agenda for a legal regulator was a radical change in 2007 and the effects are still revealing their longer term impact. The profession has therefore, since the SRA's creation, often found itself challenged by the proposals emerging from the gloriously situated offices of the SRA overlooking prime retail and restaurants outlets and high end apartments adjacent to the rejuvenated waterways of the canals in Birmingham. The SRA's location is relevant to the perspective of those who regulate you: personal injury law firms and those you contract with to market your firm's services (CMCs). The location is high-end, well-funded and often far removed from the daily practice of law. It is key therefore you develop your understanding of the SRA's thinking – as this enables you to succeed and be compliant.

The move from the Law Society Regulatory Board to the SRA under the LSA2007 was a fundamental shift and undoubtedly many issues

---

1 See the Legal Services Act 2007 Section 1 (a)

2 From https://www.sra.org.uk/sra/how-we-work.page

have a higher prominence now than previously. Whilst the LSA2007 has achieved some added consumer protections, perhaps now the SRA and the other regulators under the LSA2007 (there are fourteen (14) in total) should now be abolished and merged to create a single coherent and consistent regulatory body for consumers.

The SRA undertakes the following tasks:

1. It sets the professional standards which all firms must achieve;

2. It investigates allegations of wrongdoing;

3. It brings cases against those suspected of professional misconduct;

4. It issues guidance to solicitors and law firms to assist them in complying with the SRA Handbook;

5. It campaigns on issues which it believes protects consumers.

It is remiss of any professional not to be familiar with their guidance, but unfortunately the vast quantity of guidance can be overwhelming. This makes keeping up difficult but here are some basic tips which may help.

Inconsistent Regulation

Inconsistency hinders compliance by introducing change and creating uncertainty. Therefore, inevitably the SRA's inconsistency has been the source of some frustration within the profession since the SRA was formed and probably undermines their stated intentions. The SRA is a much maligned regulator but as the references to some of their helpful materials in later chapters shows they get many things right. Consistency is not one of them and it is a challenge they must address if they want to grow from a newly born legal regulator to a credible adult one with independence from the Law Society.

In 2007 the existing Solicitors' Handbook was revised to reflect the changes in the regulator (from the Law Society of England and Wales[3] to the SRA).

Just four years later[4], in 2011 the SRA introduced Outcomes Focused Regulation (OFR) which was intended to move regulation of law firms from solicitor centric prescriptive rules to consumer focused "*Principles*", "*Outcomes*" and "*Indicative Behaviours*"[5] . The respected legal journalist Neil Rose wrote a piece in The Guardian which summed up the objectives and the scale of the challenge for law firms in 2011 (the article remains available online for free by typing in the address within the footnote[6]).

At the time of introducing OFR the SRA stated their aims to regulate in a manner that was:

> *"proportionate, transparent and consistent"*[7]

In these simple sounding aims the SRA some might say the SRA have failed miserably as is evidenced by the fact the SRA Handbook introduced on the 6th October 2011 has been amended eighteen (18) times through to version in force from the 1st November 2016. The SRA themselves concede the current regime is flawed and plan to rewrite the rules from scratch from the Autumn of 2018 (date to be confirmed).

No Handbook for professionals should need radical change this frequently and in none of the other professions I advise in across finan-

3 Subsequently referred to as the Law Society for brevity. It is worth observing that many local Law Society's exist across England and Wales and other countries have adopted the term "Law Society of ..." to indicate a jurisdictional organisation.

4 On the 6th October 2011

5 Each of these terms is defined in later chapters as we examine how to understand what the regulator is seeking from personal injury law firms.

6 https://www.theguardian.com/law/2011/apr/07/new-rules-solicitors-ends-means1

7 The SRA assertion was made in speeches, to conferences and remains in place within their decision making guidance see https://www.sra.org.uk/sra/decision-making/guidance/investigations-decisions-investigate-concerns.page

cial services, accountancy and taxation or healthcare do their respective regulators redraft the rules with such frequency.

In fairness to the SRA it has also published much material to assist law firms and individual solicitors to comply. The volume and pace of change must, I would argue, reduce dramatically if consumers are to be protected. Throughout this book I will quote from the more useful elements and provide a link to the original source material which is available for free on the SRA website.

The fact is this book intends sometimes to translate from the SRA's objectives and guidance into understandable form so it can be understood in the context of a legal practice (rather than merely by the regulator). Showing the helicopter pilots view and then perhaps the flight path, to continue the earlier analogy.

In 2016 the SRA announced a further radical rewrite of its Handbook and associated rules to shorten the guidance. These changes were originally planned for 2017 but have been deferred until 2018 whilst amendments are made after a consultation which exposed basic errors and generated a mixed debate on the effects of the proposals. Personal injury law firms already struggling with other changes will be relieved.

TOP TIPs – How to stay up to date with the SRA requirements?

1. The SRA website has a what's new section – 10 minutes once a week will help;

2. If you are the COLP of COFA subscribe to their newsletter for Compliance Officers. It summarises key new materials;

3. At least every 6 months do a CPD course on compliance – an hour's webinar, podcast or a short course will give you the chance to think and hear a different perspective;

4. Read the Law Society's Professional Update E-Newsletter and if you are in a smaller firm their Small Firms Division E-Newslet-

ters: these are free resources which can be read quickly to give an update and pick up tips.

5. Write down on the first working day of each month what you think your biggest challenge is that month and what you are doing about it.

Increasing your knowledge and challenging your thinking by spending 30 minutes a month on this will reduce the burden and enable you to have grown your knowledge and confidence to tackle issues. Inaction is never the right option with compliance.

THE WIDER CHALLENGES – LEGISLATION, FINANCIAL AND CHANGE

What are the challenges?

My clients (law firms and solicitors across all sectors) often ask why the personal injury sector has been so badly treated by the Government, through legislation and politician's media comment and by the SRA.

The answers, like the challenges ahead, are multi-factorial and not consistent.

The Financial Crisis

The financial crisis which occurred in 2008 and led to the deepest recession in living memory affected consumers and law firms, including many personal injury law firms which relied on loans and overdrafts to pay disbursements and fund cases until the end.

The financial crisis led to unprecedented financial pressures inside many personal injury firms. It may be over but the pressures have changed firms and their operating methods.

LASPO – Funding

The Legal Aid, Sentencing and Punishment of Offenders Act 2012 (known almost universally as LASPO) change the funding options for personal injury claims radically when it came into force in April 2013.

Damages Based Agreements (DBAs) were introduced for the first time in the personal injury sector and in theory provided an alternative funding method for claimants whereby the law firm could share in the damages (up to a limit of deductions set at 25%). The take up across the sector has been poor because the 25% limit was inadequate for many law firms. Having drafted DBAs for employment law specialists for many years I have drafted a handful of DBAs for personal injury practices but the appetite for them has been limited to specific cases in the personal injury sectors rather than being a mass market. This of course contrasts with say the employment law field whereby such was their success that Employment Tribunal fees to bring a claim were introduced in 2012 to try and reduce the number of claims. Employment law DBAs are capped at 35% deduction of damages for the legal fees.

The changes to Conditional Fee Agreements were equally radical. Success fees were capped at 25% and the change to recover a 100% uplift of the law firm's costs was abolished. The main source of funding personal injury cases is now less financially attractive.

The aim was to reduce claims and the costs of the claims to the insurance sector. In contrast with the SRA's stated consumer led approach it seems the insurance industry has persuaded Parliament that the personal injury claims market needed to be curtailed.

The opportunity to reclaim After-The-Event (ATE) insurance was also lost. Many law firms used commission from ATE providers to fund the buying in of more work using referral fees. The loss of the commission coupled with the other changes has given law firms a huge compliance challenge: how to keep the fees up and grow against the reforms? The later chapters set out how this can be achieved compliantly.

LASPO – The Referral Fes Ban

The effects of Section 56 of LASPO are collectively known as the referral fee ban, the term is misleading. The ban only applies to personal injury and death related matters so solicitors in any other practice area can continue to pay referral fees. This highlights this is not about consumer protection but about the targeting of personal injury firms for objectively political reasons to tackle "excessive" "fraudulent" claims and the "compensation culture".

Section 56 is short but far from clear. The subsequent chapter on Section 56 highlights the defects in the drafting but your firm will need to review its approach when the soft tissue reform occurs in 2017/8.

In summary: specific things are banned i.e. the passing of a client's details for money. However the legislation leaves ample room for marketing your firm effectively in conjunction with a CMC or directly. Many personal injury practices acknowledge they have neither the marketing budget nor skills to compete head on with CMCs.

The number of authorised CMCs in the personal injury sector is believed to be less than 1000, down from a high of 3200 before LASPO[8].

Prison and Courts Bill 2016-2017 and the Courts Bill 2017

In February 2017 we finally saw the legislative provisions of the "whip-lash" reform. Part 5 of the draft legislation deals with the proposals. However, the draft Bill reserves key decisions to the Lord Chancellor and therefore secondary legislation is going to affect how firms interpret the Prisons and Courts Bill when it becomes an Act of Parliament.

The surprise General Election called in June 2017 saw the Prison and Courts Bill 2017 abandoned by Parliament before the election. After the election elements of the proposals were included in the new Queens

8 UK Parliament Research Briefing March 2016 http://researchbriefings.files.parliament.uk/documents/SN06075/SN06075.pdf

Speech under a new proposed act called the Courts Bill 2017. The details are awaited so cannot be dealt with here.

Change

The pace of change is the challenge for many personal injury firms. How can you take investment decisions when the rules around what CMCs can do on your behalf have changed and are still bedding in? Why would you invest in your personal injury legal business when the Government is reforming the small claims limit for personal injury reforms and whiplash (soft tissue) claims?

Uncertainty combined with change makes taking decisions difficult. The aim of some of the later chapters is to set out options for you so you can operate compliantly more easily and hence focus on the commercial effect first knowing the compliance impact is robust.

So, what is the answer?

Firms that have established a robust compliance approach and a flexible operating model which copes with change will continue to do better than most. The following chapters can help with the basics of the compliance challenge but you should also focus on the change management aspect to improve your personal injury firm's response to the challenges. Change management is about making and communicating the right decisions. Whilst that is outside the scope of this book, where they apply, points linked to change management will be mentioned.

The answer is to be flexible, be compliant and to streamline your firm's systems. The following tips should help:

1. **Involve your staff** – ideas, energy and implementation all rest with your staff. This means with any change involving them gives it a higher chance of success. It is counter intuitive for some managers to explain things rather than tell them but involving them is far more effective;

2. **Create a project team** – if for each change and challenge you create a project team the solutions (and your response) will evolve from the initial idea and will be more robust. In light of the current changes a team for the Courts Bill 2017, for the SRA's new Handbook in 2018 and for assessing and monitoring CMCs and their compliance might be 3 different project teams to make sure your firm can achieve its aim and the workload of responding is shared;

3. **Delegate** – Do not try and do everything, you will lose focus and you will drive yourself mad. Decide what can be delegated and delegate it to the project team collectively for that task or for an individual;

4. **Follow Through** – All the research shows law firms leaders are inconsistent. You need to be consistent to succeed. Write down your goal and follow through by following the steps identified. For example, Goal: Due Diligence on ABC Ltd a potential CMC. Steps: 1. Online review 2. Companies House review 3. Visit CMC and review their working methods and scripts. These steps will be developed in later chapters

5. **Stay Focused** – You need to be focused on two things: does this work commercially? Can I prove to the SRA that it is compliant?

CHAPTER THREE
THE SRA AND COMPLIANCE

This Chapter is designed to give a simple to apply summary of your professional obligations if you are regulated by the SRA. The aim is to enhance your knowledge of the basic rules, particularly those the SRA rely on when things go wrong. It's a summary of common queries and gives an overview of things. For the sake of brevity it focuses on common issues not every criteria so should be read with the SRA Handbook 2011 if tackling a problem in practice.

It is worth bearing in mind at all times that guidance from regulators can change and the Courts can reinterpret legislation and professional obligations at any time. Nothing is certain in this field. Additionally, this book is not legal advice. My publisher wants me to remind you in each Chapter that you should instruct me to give advice on your specific situation if you need it. The factual circumstances your business faces can be assessed and advised on in context which a book simply cannot do.

The SRA sets out its standards and requirements from those it regulates (individual solicitors and law firm entities) thorough the SRA Handbook 2011. Underpinning the SRA Handbook 2011 is the statutory regime which created the current regulatory framework under the Legal Services Act 2007 (LSA). Section 1 of the LSA 2007 can be paraphrased as creating a number of regulatory objectives for regulators (in the case of law firms and individual solicitors, the SRA) focused on:

- Protecting and promoting public interest considerations;
- Protecting and promoting the interests of consumers; and
- Promoting and maintaining professional standards.

Whilst Section 1 of the LSA 2007 sets out other more general obligations, anyone seeking to understand the practical implications of compliance for personal injury firms or from a management of a Claims

Management Company (CMC) perspective needs to focus on the three bullet points above.

Put bluntly, the SRA regime therefore is about the justice system and consumers, rather than the profession itself.

Five Key Elements

The SRA Handbook 2011 contains a number of regulatory elements, but for personal injury firms and CMCs, the following sections are crucial to understand the effects or to enable them to practise without problems.

A - Principles

These ten principles are mandatory and apply to all those who are regulated by the SRA (and therefore any personal injury practice will be bound by them and will need to hold any CMC they deal with to the same standards to avoid being in breach themselves).

These are fundamental, ethical and professional standards such as acting with integrity, and not undermining the rule of law. We will look at them in more detail within this chapter.

B – Code of Conduct

The Code is split into two sections containing firstly, "Outcomes" which are intended to benefit the consumers of legal services and the public at large. These are supplemented with "Indicative Behaviours" which give examples of behaviour which is typical of compliance and, confusingly in some instances, typical of non-compliance, depending on the Indicative Behaviour being cited. The purpose of introducing "Outcomes Focused Regulation" in 2011 for the SRA, was to become less prescriptive, and to focus on the individual solicitors and the law firm entities ability to comply with the standards in a variety of ways. The intended revision of the SRA Code of Conduct in 2018 demonstrates that this aim has not been achieved, as does the fact that we are currently on Version 18 of the Handbook (from 1st November 2016).

C – Accounts

The SRA Accounts Rules 2011 tend to attract the bulk of the regulatory press. Solicitors and firms who breach them inevitably end up being prosecuted before the Solicitors Disciplinary Tribunal for breaches of them.

The Rules themselves, however, are aimed at protecting client money and guiding individual practitioners on what they can, and importantly, cannot do.

D – Authorisation & Practising Requirements

These are a set of rules relating to the training admission of individuals and the requirements for setting up a law firm. This book will not focus very heavily on these. However, they are important, as on a regular basis I am instructed by those who have inadvertently breached the authorisation and practising regime and it would be remiss therefore, not to note that if you are setting up a personal injury practice, you need to ensure that each of the authorisation and practising requirements has been met. It is not enough for you to hold a Practising Certificate in your own right, the firm itself must also be authorised, as must each "Authorised Manager" such as Directors or Partners. When things change, you have 28 days under most rules to update the SRA, and when updates are in dispute, this can be contentious (example problems include when a Partner is "dismissed" from a Partnership, what date is used by the parties).

E – Client Protection

The SRA has created a set of rules around indemnity insurance, and also for compensation for certain triggering events. Again, the scope of these rules is largely outside the scope of this book, but nevertheless, an understanding of the rules can assist in avoiding problems. Rather like running a race, if you want to do well, you need to train for this. In reality that means reading the rules so they do not inadvertently catch you out.

F – Ancillary Matters

The regime contains separate rules in relation to discipline and cost recovery, practise from overseas, separate business and financial services, insolvency, and a whole section entitled "Glossary" central to all of the rules and regulations. Outside of the small cadre of professional discip-line geeks, such as myself, very few solicitors have actually read all of the rules and regimes requirements. From a practical compliance point of view therefore, we will focus on the issues coming out of sections A to C above, as these mirror the statutory obligations of the SRA in terms of consumer protection and the high risk areas for personal injury practices.

Personal Injury Practise & The SRA Principles

Whether you are a solicitor or a non-admitted member of staff, you must familiarise yourself with the SRA Principles. In this section however, I pick out the three Principles which most commonly arise in relation to personal injury work. Please do not assume that the other Principles are not important, but the emphasis in this practical guide is on common problems.

Principle 2 - You Must Act with Integrity

Principle 2 is a wide-ranging obligation which is deemed central to the role of solicitors as clients' trusted advisors, and therefore, all interactions with clients, with the Courts, other lawyers, and the public must be subject to the Principle of Integrity.

In practise, what this means is that you must not act in a morally ambiguous manner.

The case law suggests that dishonesty and integrity, whilst often linked, are not intrinsically linked, and the obligation under Principle 2 has therefore been more widely interpreted to be about wider conduct over and above that involving dishonesty. The debate over the link between dishonesty and integrity is likely to vex the Courts for many years yet not least as the proposed SRA Code of Conduct 2018 uses both words in a single Principle.

Principle 3 – You Must Not Allow Your Independence to be Compromised

A solicitor's ability to give advice which is focused purely on the client's best interests should not be fettered.

This of course applies to non-admitted staff working under the supervision of a solicitor as well. It is not uncommon in the personal injury sector, where an individual under a solicitor's supervision allows their independence to be inhibited by, for example, an external party, or a friend or relative, this compromises not only them, but the firm, and their supervising solicitor's independence.

In essence, independence under the scope of the SRA Principles means not requiring the authority or conceding control to any other person or body.

The SRA give the example of handing over control of your practice or a case to someone who is outside of the SRA regime. Whilst at first flush this may seem fanciful, the cases over recent years before the Solicitors Disciplinary Tribunal have seen, for financial reasons, law firms permit influence and control by those not recorded as having such influence or control under the regime established by the LSA 2007.

Ask yourself:

- Who wants to know what?
- Why?
- Could this be seen as controlling or influencing me?

Principle 4 – You Must Act in the Best Interest of Each Client

The SRA perceives two major challenges to Principle 4 and acting in the best interest of clients. Firstly, with regards to the duty of confidentiality to the clients, this comes before anything else. For personal injury firms therefore, sharing information about the status of the case with a CMC, or updating funding partners, requires express consent. The obligation is to put the client's interests ahead of any introducer's wishes or needs. In the personal injury sphere, this has caused numerous problems and challenges, and you may encounter CMCs being resistant to this approach, but client's interests must come first.

Case Study – CFA Costs

Counsel in a CFA case may want an update on the case every month after providing written advice. This is permitted only with the client's consent. This means you should seek it. Alternatively, for billing purposes Counsel cannot know! You may need to explain this to Counsel of course.

The second major area is with regard to conflicts of interest. Law firms and their managers must constantly ask themselves if there is a conflict, either of their own interest with the clients (particularly pertinent in relation to matters funded under a Conditional Fee Agreement), or that of another client, for example, bringing claims for two claimants involved in the same accident at different times.

Firms are expected to evidence how they have avoided both their own interests, and that of other clients from inhibiting what is best for each and every single client.

Practical Tips:

- Record on your case management software opening page that no conflicts exist after a search.
- Add a box to confirm that no conflict with the firm's interests is known.

Principle 6 – Behaving in a Way that Maintains the Trust the Public Places in You, Your Firm, and Generally in the Provision of Legal Services

The SRA when considering disciplinary action are very keen to include allegations in relation to Principle 6. Their focus is on the conduct, whether it is inside, or outside of practise which may damage public trust in the legal profession as a whole within society. This potentially could be far wider than at first glance, and in recent cases, has involved misplaced humour that ended up in the public domain through email trails, or comments in public or on social media which affected public perception. The acid test I advise my clients to adopt is:

> *"If you are a member of the public and you heard about certain conduct or behaviours, would it undermine your trust in you:*
>
> - *as an individual; or*
> - *in the profession?"*

If the answer is yes to either of those questions, or both of those questions, then it is conduct which potentially breaches Principle 6.

Other Principles

Other Principles include upholding the rule of law, providing a proper standard of service to clients, being cooperative with the SRA and other regulators (including the Legal Ombudsman), promoting equality and diversity, running your business in an effective manner, and protecting client money and assets.

Firms engaging in an aggressive or litigious manner with the Legal Ombudsman (LeO) for example, may breach this and hinder their credibility with the LeO.

How are the Principles Used by the SRA?

When contemplating enforcement, the SRA apply the particular circumstances arising to the allegation of a breach of one of the Principles. How they apply it varies from case to case. When conducting advisory work before the SRA are involved therefore, I try and encourage clients to build their awareness of how those Principles arise in their day-to-day activities. For conflicts of interest, for example, this includes thinking beyond a conflict of interest search against other clients, but it is contemplating whether or not the firm's own interests may at some stage play a part in advising on, for example, a settlement which would bring money into the firm in terms of the payment of costs more quickly than would otherwise be the case. It may also arise when selecting a particular expert, where perhaps there is a family connection. In such circumstances, having a log of the reasoning for your decision is crucial. I strongly advocate logging such matters, both on the individual client's file, and also placing a copy of that note in a central register.

It is important for personal injury practices to demonstrate all third party relationships they naturally require such as medical agencies, experts, providers of complimentary services, such as car hire, physiotherapy, After The Event insurance, do not impair their ability to comply with the Principles. If in any doubt, then ask yourself what would I say if the SRA asked me to evidence why this was appropriate? That should be noted down and stored. If you cannot answer the question to your own satisfaction after the event, satisfying the SRA would be almost impossible.

Practical Tip:

- Keep an Excel spreadsheet of your decision reasons. For most COLP's/COFA's this is a five minute a day job. It demonstrates that critical review and thinking exists however.

Code of Conduct 2011

The structure of the SRA Code of Conduct is relatively informative. The Code is divided into five sections as follows:

Section 1 – You and your client

This focuses on the relationship between an individual solicitor and the firm and its clients. This is broken down into six chapters consisting of the following:

<u>Chapter One – Client Care</u>

The obligations within this chapter are around providing a proper standard of service, taking into account the individual needs and circumstances of each client. In other words, taking a generic or factory farming approach to clients is a high risk strategy but it is a strategy that is often pursued by personal injury practices.

Key challenges I see from these obligations on a regular basis are treating clients fairly and allegations that clients have not been treated in a fair manner are relatively common. The obligation to provide the service to the clients in a confident and timely manner is also subject to interpretation and misinterpretation, and on a regular basis I see personal injury practices within their client information, making the information regarding complaints and their rights to complain, and particularly around the Legal Ombudsman, either impossible to locate or being omitted altogether.

- Does what you are doing pass the "this client test"? In other words, generic answers are not good enough. Each individual client's interests must be put first.
- Do you have the appropriate skills, resources and procedures to undertake this client's instructions?

- Is the way in which the matter funded particularly any fee arrangements, suitable for the client's matter, and in the client's (and not the firm's) best interests?

- Are clients informed in writing at the outset about their right to complain and how complaints may be made?

Whilst these themes are non-exhaustive, and you should familiarise yourself with the entirety of Chapter One, focusing on these four issues will inevitably enhance your compliance with Chapter One.

In the personal injury sector, when the SRA come calling, those are the key issues which have been arising for a number of years, so the challenge to evidence compliance to avoid disciplinary sanction is well known. However the themes for the SRA are subject to change and you should not ignore the wider points.

<u>Chapter Two – Equality and Diversity</u>

One of the most controversial aspects arising from the SRA's obligations under the LSA 2007 is the increased emphasis on encouraging equality of opportunity and respect for protected characteristics under the Equality Act 2010 (these are age, disability, gender reassignment, marriage and civil partnership, maternity and pregnancy, race, religion or belief, sex and sexual orientation). In essence, through your systems and processes you must ensure that clients and colleagues and suppliers are not subject to any inappropriate behaviour, or any inappropriate policy, practice, or criteria.

Practical Tips:

- If your clients have learning difficulties, what process do you have in place to identify and manage their needs?

- In relation to potentially vulnerable clients (such as those with learning difficulties and children) what policies and training do you have to ensure they can access your services and are not prejudiced by any characteristics such as age or the learning difficulty?

- What process and policies do you have in place to prevent discriminatory conduct towards people of different race or sex? For example, do you only instruct full time members of the Bar? If so, this could inadvertently prejudice women which tend to be more frequently part-time? Whilst this is indirect discrimination potentially, your process of selecting Counsel purely on their legal expertise rather than their working pattern could avoid any such criticism.

I indicated above that the equality and diversity obligation has been controversial. It has been controversial because the SRA Code of Conduct 2011 for the first time, has relied upon the express obligations. The obligations which arise generally under the Equality Act 2010 are, in the eyes of many, sufficient and the SRA is merely confusing matters by going beyond legal compliance due to its diversity agenda.

Chapter Three – Conflicts of Interest

You can never act where there is a conflict, or a significant risk of conflict, between you and your client. In practise, this means that if at the outset of a matter your interests and a client's have a significant risk of a conflict, then *you must decline those instructions*.

Where there is a conflict, or a significant risk of conflict, between two or more current clients, you must not act for all or both of them, unless the matter falls outside the scope of the limited exceptions set out in Chapter Three.

In terms of practical tips, running a conflict search prior to taking on a matter is essential and this being recorded on the file (electronically or on paper).

Recording why it is appropriate to take a matter on and keeping records of any matters declined centrally provides good evidence of your compliance with this obligation.

Chapter Four – Confidentiality and Disclosure

The protection of confidential information is an essential characteristic of the relationship between a solicitor (and thus a law firm) and their clients. Confidentiality as a duty exists as both a matter of law (legal professional privilege), and as a matter of conduct (under the Code of Conduct 2011). The law firms caught up in the "Panama Papers" scandal in 2016 demonstrated how an issue can suddenly arise due to external factors. The outcome is unknown as yet as worldwide regulators continue to investigate.

The duty continues even at the end of the solicitor-client retainer, and even in the event of the client subsequently dying.

The duties of conduct are wider than the concept of law known as Legal Professional Privilege (LPP). Your fee earning staff should be able to distinguish between confidentiality and LPP. If you are not sure they can, you should provide training to them on this point.

Practical tips:

- Ensure that each and every member of staff has been trained, including support staff, consultants and locums, that they owe a duty of confidentiality towards your clients? If you cannot evidence this training and there is a confidentiality breach, you as a law firm manager or individual solicitor may be liable.

- If in personal injury matters you share information, including about the progress of a case, with your CMCs, or any other third parties, you need express written consent from the client to share this information. In practical terms, no information should be shared without a written authority. This written authority should make clear that the client can cancel the authority for future disclosures at any time without notice and with immediate effect.

- It is essential that if you are a law firm manager, that you are reminding your staff of their duties with regards to confidentiality and disclosure to third parties at least annually.

- The forthcoming General Data Protection Regulation (GDPR) regime will amend the Data Protection Act 1998 (by repeating elements) and increase the consent threshold when sharing data. Are you ready? Are your teams?

Chapter Five – Your Client and the Court

Whether you are conducting litigation, or conducting advocacy, you have duties to the Court. Fundamentally, you must not attempt to deceive or knowingly or recklessly mislead the Court (Outcome 5.1), but your duties are wider than that and include an obligation not to assist in any other person deceiving or misleading the Court, and in complying with court orders which place obligations upon you as an individual professional (or your firm).

Practical Tips:

Ensure that all staff are aware of their duties to the Court as follows:

- Ensure all staff (including locums and consultants and non-admitted staff) are aware that the duties to the Court outweigh their obligations to the client. The obligations towards the Court must therefore take precedence where they conflict.

- Ensure that all fee earning staff understand that they must not construct facts to support the client's case or assist the client in constructing facts to support the case. Again, training records should be at least annual on this point.

- Ensure that your fee earning staff know that they must not suggest that a person is guilty of a crime, fraud, or misconduct unless such allegations go to the heart of the client's own case and appear to be supported by reasonable grounds.

- These training issues repeatedly arise in personal injury matters in relation to staff seeking to promote the client's best interests but forgetting the wider obligation to the Court. Training, particularly repeat training, is the only way to manage this risk in my view.

Chapter Six – Your Client and Introduction to Third Parties

All professionals have occasions when they want to, because it is in the client's interests, refer those clients to third parties, either perhaps another lawyer (such as counsel, or where there is a conflict of interest), or to another service provider (whether that be financial services to ensure they are properly advised on how to handle any cash receive, or in personal injury cases, medical experts or car service providers).

Fundamental to your duties is that whenever you recommend such a service, it is in the client's best interests and does not compromise independence. You must be able to evidence this if asked to do so.

Practical tips:

- Evidence on each and every file that clients are fully informed of any financial or other interest which you may have in referring the client to another person or business (declaring this clearly and in writing).
- Ensure that you are not paid and are not paying a prohibited referral fee (as defined by the Legal Aid, Sentencing and Punishment of Offenders Act 2012).
- Maintain records to ensure that you can demonstrate that any payments you receive are not prohibited referral fees and have been fully accounted for to clients.

Section 2 – You and Your Business

The second of the five sections of the Code is you and your business. At first glance it may appear that some of the obligations in this section do not apply to all staff, or indeed, only apply to those involved in the management of a business. Whilst this impression is largely true, there are quirky exemptions to this and having advised those who have been caught out my impression is beware the quirks.

In the personal injury sector, the quirks have led to a number of controversies. These controversies tend to have focused on publicity which does not necessarily of course have to involve managers. Social media and online advertising have changed the risks and the environment for all law firms, but personal injury solicitors have been the focus of the Advertising Standards Authority decisions to date in relation to "No Win No Fee" advertising, so those making decisions could be non-lawyer staff, managers (in an Alternative Business Structure (ABS)), or marketing professionals expert in marketing, but perhaps failing to see the SRA implications.

Chapter 7 - Management of Your Business

This chapter focuses on having clear and effective governance structures and reporting lines. Most importantly, it focuses on the need for firms to train individuals to maintain a level of competence appropriate to their work level and their responsibility. It also prevents the outsourcing of legal activities or operational functions that are crucial to the delivery of legal services. This restricts what can be outsourced and what cannot be outsourced, which can be a major issue for personal injury practices who are trying to streamline their practices moving forward, with the reduction in fees discussed in previous chapters.

In terms of practical tips, the following are often useful:

- Have a Risk Register dealing with how you manage and supervise your workloads. If you do not have a review of the risks on at least a quarterly basis, how do you evidence that your managing risk as the SRA require?

- Train your supervisors in the skill of supervision. The analogy I always draw is lots of us who watch football games think our reading of a football game is better than half the managers managing in the FA Premiership. How many of us though, are qualified as football coaches to a sufficient level that we could manage a team in the Premiership? Similarly, your supervisors should be trained in the skill of supervision. At least annually, supervisors should be trained on supervision and getting the best from their subordinates.

Chapter 8 - Publicity

Publicity should not be misleading, and if it contains anything which may be controversial, you will want to consider carefully whether or not that is appropriate. The ASA has made a number of rulings in relation to law firms, some of which have upheld complaints against them when the ASA have believed that the publicity was misleading, and others where the ASA have supported the law firms where they have been able to evidence the claims made, such as success rates or average value of claims.

With claims in advertising and publicity materials everything starts from what does the evidence say?

In terms of practical tips for personal injury firms, the following should be at the forefront of your minds:

- The opted-in data or consent used to approach an individual about bringing a new personal injury claim should be traceable from your law firm back to the opt in point. If you acquire business from CMCs, how do you evidence to the SRA that they had consent to make the approach? You should be seeking evidence that those referred to you can be demonstrably shown to have consented to being contacted.

- Reviewing at least 10% of claims received from CMCs by asking for evidence of the consent to receive the marketing undertaken is a good starting point.

- Reviewing the claims made about success on your own website is essential. This should be done at least quarterly, and the pages should be printed out and confirmed. If your website is static i.e. you are not updating it on a regular basis, this can be less so, but static websites attract less traffic, and therefore, what purpose does your website have?

Chapter 9 – Fee Sharing and Referrals

The relationship between solicitors and their law firms and third parties is of fundamental interest to the SRA due to their consumer protection obligations. Historically, personal injury firms have created numerous third party arrangements, and over recent years, I have seen challenges to these in almost every SRA investigation I have advised on.

The fundamental principle is that your independence and professional judgement should not be seen to be impaired, or be impaired, by virtue of any relationship with any third party.

Perception and reality matter. The SRA, without a commercial angle, often simply see problems, **not** the client benefit.

Fundamental to avoiding problems is that any financial or other interest which arises as a consequence of the relationship is declared. Common problems such as not declaring shareholdings or profit share arrangements are widely reported. A common issue is that clients are informed very often, but are informed as part of a clause in a lengthy document, and therefore, the communication itself is not effective and the link between the parties is ambiguous.

Practical tips to consider include:

- You must have a written agreement whenever you have a financial arrangement or introducer. Audit your current arrangements. If you do not have a written agreement for any reason, whether it is because of a family connection or marriage for example, put one in place immediately. Mandatory Outcome 9.7 requires this irrespective of any relationship, including two separate entities being controlled by the same individual (such as a law firm and CMC controlled by the same owner).

- Ensure that your declaration of any financial or other interest is clear and unambiguous. Ideally, have the client sign to confirm receipt of the same.

- When working with CMCs, record any comments about the CMC centrally so that these can be assessed monthly by the Compliance Officer for Legal Practice (COLP) and Compliance Officer for Finance and Administration (COFA). The obligation not to accept clients that have been pressurised or misled into instructing you, arising under Indicative Behaviour 9.12, is best evidenced by contemporary periodic evidence. One solution can be for first response staff to have a special CMC feedback internal email address where they can just quickly write a one line email about any feedback. Looking at the patterns in that feedback monthly for Compliance Officers can help demonstrate that working with the CMC is not undermining public confidence in both the law firm, and the legal sector more generally. It also allows early patterns to be spotted, by having all data in one space.

Section 3 – You and Your Regulator

The third section of the Handbook is entitled You and Your Regulator. This is wider than simply the SRA, and includes any other regulators with whom you may come into contact, such as the Legal Ombudsman (LeO) and the Information Commissioners Office (ICO).

Practical tips include the following:

- Notify the SRA within seven days of any changes to personnel within the business in terms of those that are registered with the SRA. Early notification when an Authorised Manager or Compliance Officer leaves is essential to ensure the SRA have confidence in you to appoint a replacement. In the case of Compliance Officers, you have 28 days to replace them.

- In any response to the SRA or LeO, ensure that your actions are open and transparent. This does not mean that you should admit any wrongdoing. Factually however, you must set out the facts. The interpretation of those facts you do not need to set out. Seek specialist advice before you make any admission (the effects are long term).

- Ensure that you do not attempt to prevent anyone from providing information to the SRA or LeO. Often, when employees and partners are in dispute, the suggestion is that they are pressurised into not sharing information with the SRA and Legal Ombudsman. This is best avoided, not only because it is a mandatory Outcome (10.7), but also because it is counterproductive, and it is far better to be open and transparent and engage with the SRA to minimise the effects of any aggrieved person's comments.

- Ensure that training for your Compliance Officers is provided on a regular basis. I would recommend at least every six months an update should occur on the SRA's Agenda. This could take the form of a webinar, attending a half day or full day seminar, or attending SRA compliance events.

Section 4 – You and Others

The fourth section of the Handbook focuses on the relationship both with third parties, and with any other separate businesses.

The issue of giving and receiving undertakings is covered by this part. It is always worth reminding practitioners that there is no obligation to give or receive an undertaking on behalf of a client, but if you do, you must ensure that you are in a position to discharge that undertaking. For those engaged in conveyancing, undertakings are an almost daily occurrence, but for those in other areas of law, including personal injury, undertakings are rarely given, and can therefore be a more high risk option. It makes sense for the provision of undertakings to be limited to one or two experienced members of your team. For a sole practitioner, that is easy to achieve in theory, but of course, some sole practitioners may engage 100 to 200 staff within the personal injury sector, and therefore, training them on what they can and cannot do, and what is and is not an undertaking, is crucial.

Undertakings – Much wider than you think!

An undertaking is a statement, whether given orally or in writing, whether or not it includes the word "undertake" or "undertaking", which is made by or on behalf of you or your firm which someone else reasonably places reliance on that you, or your firm, will do something or cause to be done some action, or will refrain from doing something.

My advice to clients when asked 'is this an undertaking?' Could someone reasonably rely that you were going to do or not do something? If the answer is yes, then it is an undertaking and should be recording within your undertaking register.

Chapter 11 – Relations With Third Parties

Of primary importance is not taking advantage of any third parties in either your professional or personal capacity. In other words, if somebody is a litigant in person on the other side to you, you should not take advantage of them. A common complaint is that communication with other law firms' clients has occurred without authorisation. Training your team, therefore, not to make contact where somebody has retained a lawyer, except to request the name and address of the other party's lawyer, or where for some unusual reason you have express consent (recorded in writing) from the lawyer to communicate with their client i.e. on an unrelated issue.

In terms of practical tips, think of the following:

- Have a centralised undertakings register.

- Remind your team at least annually of their obligation not to take unfair advantage of an opposing parties lack of legal knowledge.

This is particularly key when non-admitted staff may be having the majority of contact with third parties.

- Ensure that your staff are trained at least annually not to demand anything for themselves or on behalf of their client which is not legally recoverable i.e. seeking expenses which are not legally recoverable at the stage reached.

Chapter 12 – Separate Businesses

The SRA's regime for separate businesses recently changed. If you have a separate business, you should read their guidance on separate businesses, and you should ensure that no clients could be confused as to when you are acting in a separate business and when you are acting in your law firm capacity.

Solicitors Accounts Rules 2011

Like the SRA Handbook, the current version of the Solicitors Accounts Rules will be abolished and replaced probably during the course of 2018. The underlying principles, however, will largely remain the same in that the emphasis will remain on protecting client money and protecting client assets. The obligations to act with integrity and to behave in a way that maintains the public trust in how solicitors handle client funds will remain the same as the principles, but the detailed rules will change which will dramatically affect how personal injury practices can handle money moving forward. However, given that these rules have yet to be finalised, looking only at the current regime, the following practical tips may be useful under the current regime.

Practical Tips:

- In relation to client money, it must be returned to the client (or any other person on behalf of which the money is held) promptly, as soon as there is no longer a proper reason to retain those funds. A number of firms in recent years have got into difficulty when they have held on to monies at the end of their instruction and have failed to return the money either to the client, or in personal injury firms cases, make a refund to insurers where the client has lost contact with the firm. Ask yourself if you have any balances which are over six months old in credit on a client account, and if so, the funds should either be returned to the client, or if this is not practical, returned to the insurers pending further contact with the client. At first this can seem odd, but the second point clarifies why below.

- Under Rule 14.5, you must not provide a banking facility through your client account. This, in practice, is causing much difficulty to law firms, and there have been a number of high profile banking facility cases, including some I have been involved in as advocate, which have attracted widespread publicity. What you understand as banking, and what the SRA understands as banking, probably do not match. Training your staff on what a banking facility is under Rule 14.5 is therefore essential. Payments into, transfers and withdrawals from the client account must be in respect of an underlying legal transaction (such as a personal injury claim) and form a normal part of your regulated activities (such as litigation).

- Payments to third parties on behalf of the client because they claim not to have a bank account etc. should be avoided. Making payments on behalf of a client to a third party is potentially providing a banking service, and therefore, until the SRA give a definition of banking facilities, given that it is not defined either in their rules, or in the Financial Services and Markets Act 2000, it should be a normal part of your regulated activities if you are making the payment to any third parties i.e. expert witnesses etc.

- You should have a written policy on the payment of interest which seeks to provide a fair outcome to the client. The payment of interest is not required where the amount payable is below a de minimis level, but this must be set at a reasonable level and regularly reviewed in light of current interest rates. Therefore, record your reason for setting the required level to attract interest payments in your risk register.

Section 5 – Authorisation and Practising Requirements

The fifth and final component part consists of the rules which authorise how firms are regulated.

The common challenges to personal injury firms include firms setting up or updating their partners or authorised managers and not doing so in accordance with the rules. It is outside the scope of this book to focus on this in detail, but the following two tips may assist:

- Ensure that no person holds themselves out as a director of your law firm unless they have been authorised to act as an "Authorised Manager" or director by the SRA in advance.
- Ensure the SRA are notified within the 28 day period required under the SRA Authorisation Rules 2011 of any changes to the partnership. Best practice advice would be to notify them within seven days, meaning that if there is any problem emerging, you have a further 21 days to resolve the same. In practise the SRA normally respond within five to seven days to such notifications, and therefore, you probably have in practice, 10 to 14 days to find a solution if anything proves problematic.

General Good Habits

The SRA regime is, as set out above, designed to protect clients. Part of this is that you should be conducting due diligence on any staff that you hire and anybody who will have access to your confidential information.

Therefore, the following practical tips are useful for every firm in the country:

- Seek to ensure that any prospective member of staff's name is checked against the SRA Decision Register. This can be found at www.sra.org.uk/consumers/solicitor-check.page. You can search by an individual's name and an individual's SRA ID. It is important to remember that non-admitted staff can be subject to prohibitions to prevent them from working in law firms moving forward.

- Take references from any previous employer. Staff who leave one law firm and go to another may bring with them problems. If you are taking a reference from another firm of solicitors, you are minimising the opportunity for criticism of your recruitment process by the SRA if that problem does occur within your firm.

- Have a rolling compliance training programme for all your staff and in particular, your Authorised Managers under the SRA regime and your COLPs and your COFAs. This regime should be targeted to the type of work that you do and the type of client base that you operate. You should record why you have made the decision to target your training in that way.

Conclusion

The SRA are not there, contrary to popular myth, to catch practitioners out or to be deliberately obstructive. They are, however, there to focus on public protection rather than professional protection. Once this is accepted as a concept, it becomes easier to allocate a small amount of time each week to deal with management and compliance issues. By having a set period of time when you address these points, you avoid the risk that your fee earning work always take precedent and compliance tasks do not get completed.

If you cannot afford to step back from fee earning and you are involved in the running of your law firm, you must have a golden period of time which is uninterrupted to focus on the compliance issues. You must record your decisions, and using a daily log can be a useful way of doing this. A daily log may consist of only one or two lines every day, but it will demonstrate that you are thinking about compliance and the issues arising in day-to-day practise should a problem subsequently emerge. Even recording "no issues arising today" can be useful some years later when asked "Why did you do that?" The answer may be we were not informed of that fact as per the client file and daily compliance log.

CHAPTER FOUR
CLAIMS MANAGEMENT REGULATOR (CMR) RULES OVERVIEW

Introduction

The CMR manages the conduct of CMCs through the Conduct of Authorised Persons Rules 2014 and some other additional guidance issued from time to time, primarily, the Client Account Rules 2006 for CMCs that handle client's money, which is likely to be rare in cases when a law firm is also involved. The major addition to the Conduct of Authorised Persons Rules 2014 which will usually apply is the Marketing and Advertising Guidance for CMCs, published on 1 April 2014. In this Chapter, we will concentrate on the Conduct of Authorised Persons Rules 2014 as they always apply and are the underlying dominant force in how the CMCs that your law firm is working with should be undertaking their work. In relation to the marketing guidance in each of the other chapters we have covered key elements of those rules in a practical manner, albeit, on a topic by topic approach rather than by addressing the collective rules.

It is worth bearing in mind at all times that guidance from regulators can change and the Courts can reinterpret legislation and professional obligations at any time. Nothing is certain in this field. Additionally, this book is not legal advice. My publisher wants me to remind you in each Chapter that you should instruct me to give advice on your specific situation if you need it. The factual circumstances your business faces can be assessed and advised on in context which a book simply cannot do.

Conduct of Authorised Persons Rules 2014: The Format

The format over the course of twelve pages, including a covering page, back page, and contents page, is simple, principle, based guidance. This guidance is split into two key areas as follows:

a) General rules dealing with the principles, the conduct of business, complaints and redress, monitoring and compliance and disciplinary arrangements, and issues surrounding data protection and regulatory matters;

b) Client specific rules focused around general principles, advertising and marketing and rules on representing a client.

The Rules came into force from 1 October 2014 and could be updated at any stage by the CMR who have the statutory right to amend their rules pursuant to Regulation 22 of the Compensation (Claims Management Services) Regulations 2006.

The Rules are stated as applying to all CMCs and superseding any previous rules issued.

General Rules

There is no better way to make yourself familiar with the Rules than to study the entire Rules collectively, given their short nature, but the following Rules are particularly pertinent to working with CMCs effectively from a law firm's perspective, despite of course the law firm being governed by the SRA regime. This is because in any investigation the SRA would expect evidence of verification of compliance.

Honesty and Integrity

Principle 1 of the General Rules requires that a CMC shall conduct itself with honesty and integrity. These are words which have much vexed professional disciplinary Tribunals and the High Court in relation to professional disciplinary matters. There is an ongoing debate amongst professional disciplinary lawyers as to whether or not honesty and integrity are one and the same thing, or are distinct. My advice is to treat them as distinct with integrity being a general obligation to conduct the business in a straightforward and upright manner, and honesty for the CMC as being acting in a manner free of deceit or untruthfulness, and in a fair manner.

Despite the extensive case law in relation to solicitors, doctors and barristers surrounding honesty and integrity, there is no guidance on the meaning of the words from the CMR, and therefore, applying the strict dictionary definitions or the simplified version of the same outlined above would be sensible. Ask yourself:

a) Is your CMC conducting itself honestly?

b) Is it misleading consumers?

c) Is everything it does to generate leads for you done with integrity?

As a law firm, if you are not satisfied with regards to your CMCs Principle 1 compliance, then you should not be acting with them in a commercial relationship.

Conduct Itself Responsibly

The second principle consists of additional obligations set out in 2 a) to f) which can be summarised as investigating a claim to make sure it has merits, making representations to a third party (defendant or insurer) which it cannot substantiate, not pursuing false, fraudulent or misleading claims, complying with any ombudsman obligations, maintaining records and audit trails, and taking all reasonable steps to ensure that any referrals, leads or data have been obtained in accordance with the requirements of legislation and rules (by which it means the CMR's own rules and the ICO's rules), and having procedures in place for the early identification of vulnerable consumers.

As a law firm, you can assess the merits and the quality of the leads that you receive. This allows you to assess whether or not the CMC is complying with Principle 2 a).

Similarly, if you have concerns regarding fraudulent, false or misleading claims, these will quickly become apparent, and again, as a matter of course, you should distance yourself from any CMC generating these. Whilst an occasional isolated claim will give rise to concern, if there is a pattern or a spate of claims which you believe are fraudulent, false or misleading, then, inevitably, it causes you to question whether or not that commercial relationship is appropriate, or whether it needs to be suspended or terminated until the CMC has improved its systems and processes sufficiently to avoid repetition of introductions to potentially fraudulent, false or misleading claims.

The obligation to take all reasonable steps in relation to complying with the obligations on referrals, leads and data is a deliberately wide ranging one. Your commercial relationship (contract) with your CMCs should, inevitably, give you the right to terminate if any of the rules have been broken in this regard. This is both the CMR's and the SRA's general investigation area in relation to CMCs and law firms working with CMCs, and having an audit trail proving those arrangements, in terms of the origin of the data, are robust, is essential, as is set out in the Checklist Chapter which follows later in this book.

In relation to vulnerable consumers, vulnerability can come through mental health, a physical or mental disability, partially sighted, deaf, or even elderly and vulnerable to persuasion, and a CMC should be ensuring that they are not pursuing claims on behalf of vulnerable consumers through a law firm, or indeed, directly if they are authorised to undertake the work directly. As a law firm dealing with a CMC, you should ask to see their Vulnerable Persons Policy and training materials, and you should satisfy yourself that it provides an adequate gateway to claims being referred on to you from potentially vulnerable consumers. This does not mean that vulnerable consumers should be excluded from accessing your services (as this would potentially in some cases breach the Equality Act 2010 where there is a disability), but it does mean that such vulnerable persons must be treated appropriately as clients with appropriate safeguards in place to ensure they are not taken advantage of, either by the CMC, or indeed, your law firm.

Competence

Principles 3 and 4 relate to both the people running the business (the directors and shadow directors), and the staff having the necessary training and competence. For those directing the business, it means having a working knowledge of the legislation and rules, and to that end, when you are contemplating working with a CMC as a law firm, you should be asking what training and what experience they have of complying with the CMC rules, and you should be documenting their responses and taking copies of any training that they have received as part of your due diligence into matters.

If there is a contracting party who is not a director establish who they are and what their status is. If in doubt, do not contract with that CMC. Shadow directors are a potential minefield so treat absence from the official registers of Companies House and the CMR with great caution.

Principle 5 is a catchall that the CMC shall observe "all laws and regulations" which are relevant to the business of the CMC. It is, again, deliberately wide-ranging in order to ensure that those operating CMCs have very limited wiggle room and the issue of their compliance (more pertinently their non-compliance) arises.

Conduct of Business

Principle 6 requires that when applying for authorisation, and then annually when completing its annual return to the CMR that the business confirms it shall comply and has complied with the obligations placed on it by the regime. When working with a new potential supplier which is a CMC, you should ask to see both its initial application for authorisation, and check the details therein with the published details against the CMR's current registration (including as to whether or not there are any investigations ongoing), and their last annual return to the CMR. Copies of these documents should be retained demonstrating that you have, as a law firm, considered their compliance.

For the CMC, the purpose of certifying annually that they have complied is to make non-compliance enforcement easier, and it is therefore a protective step from the regulator.

Complaints

CMCs in terms of complaints are potentially subject to two regimes. Firstly and primarily, the Legal Ombudsman has had jurisdiction since January 2015 for CMC complaints. Secondly, the ICO will have jurisdiction in relation to the use (and misuse) of data, irrespective of whether the CMC is registered with the ICO pursuant to the Data Protection Act 1998. With the forthcoming General Data Protection Rule (GDPR) due to come into place in May 2018, the obligations towards the Information Commissioner's Office will be unaffected in terms of jurisdiction, but the obligations as data handlers will, as with all other data handlers, be heightened by the enhanced regime which is coming into force.

Law firms dealing with CMCs on or after the introduction of GDPR would be well advised to review their CMCs GDPR planning three months prior to the introduction of GDPR in May 2018, and at the time that it comes into force, should make a note of any changes to systems or processes so that these can be verified, either by the SRA if they audit the law firm, or alternatively, if any problems are likely to arise, that they can be addressed by their commercial partner as a matter of urgency. Clearly, not being in compliance with the legislation once it comes into force will be a serious matter with enhanced financial penalties, and law firms accepting work from CMCs in breach of GDPR are likely to face investigation and sanction from the ICO.

Conclusion – General Rules

The General Rules are not all addressed in the comments above, and there is no substitute for reading them, but the key challenges are fleshed out with some guidance beyond the mere words on the page from the CMR. This Chapter should, however, be read in conjunction with the CMR's Conduct of Authorised Persons Rules 2014.

Client Specific Rules

These rules set out how a CMC should conduct itself and must be complied with at all stages. CMCs are required to keep evidence to demonstrate, where practical, that it has complied with the rules. This obligation to retain evidence of compliance is, of course, a potentially rich source of due diligence for law firms working with CMCs, and it should become part of a normal review process to access it.

General Principles

Principle 1 requires broadly a CMC to act fairly and reasonably, and to ensure that the services offered meet the needs of the client, and that all information given to the client is in a clear, transparent, fair and not misleading manner. An obligation to avoid conflicts of interest and to preserve confidentiality is also created by Principle 1 a) to f) of the client specific rules.

From a law firm's perspective, the key thing is the audit and training in relation to these measures, rather than the details of the rules themselves. Is the CMC you are planning on dealing with able to demonstrate that it is meeting the requirements of Principle 1 a) to f)? If it is, you should have no concern about dealing with them. If they have not kept an audit trail, then you should require them to create one and to maintain one as part of a pre-requisite condition to dealing with them.

Advertising, Marketing and Soliciting Business

Principle 2 requires that all advertising, marketing and other soliciting must conform to the Codes of Practice in place and published by The Committee of Advertising Practice (CAP), whose Codes can be found at www.cap.org.uk/advertising-codes.aspx.

This will apply to telesales, promotional material, and the CMCs own website. Each must comply with the CAP Codes.

Principle 3 strictly prohibits high pressure selling. There is no clear definition of high pressure selling, but in essence, a law firm should be alert to suggestions from clients once they have been received from the CMC that they were pressurised into potentially making a claim. Any CMCs which conduct themselves in this manner, except on a very isolated basis i.e. one in every thousand, or where there is a potential pattern of allegations from consumers of high pressure selling, should distance themselves by terminating their relationship with the CMC involved. The key is to evidence, through scripts from the CMCs that demonstrate high pressure selling does not happen and is not encouraged by the CMC. This will increase the need for CMCs to demonstrate that their staff do not go off any prepared scripts as part of their sales process. As in other areas where high pressure selling has been alleged in the past, it is likely that there will be regulator interest, and common examples are things like mis-sold financial products and electronic devices. Obviously the outcomes in terms of the statutory regimes behind it means this is unlikely to lead to large compensation pay-outs unlike other mis-selling areas, but any CMC engaging in high pressure selling risks bringing the law firm into disrepute.

Cold Calling

Cold calling is strictly prohibited. Any marketing whether by telephone, email, fax or text shall be governed by the DMA's Code and, of course, the guidance issued by the ICO including the guidance on the PECR to which a chapter of this book is dedicated.

Principle 5 is a strict prohibition on the use of leaflets advertising in public buildings and medical facilities to avoid what the tabloid press would described as, 'ambulance chasing' under promotion of services unless the management of that building or facility has authorised such advertising.

Advertising Standards

Principle 6 requires that any advertising or marketing identifies the name of the advertiser, does not offer any cash incentive or similar inducement to make a claim, does not promote the idea that a compensation payment may be used in a way that it is not consistent with the cause of the claim and does not imply that the business is approved by the government or in any way connected with any government agency or regulator. The CMR guides that a business that wishes to mention that it is authorised may only use the following words which must be used in their entirety:

> *"Regulated by the Claims Management Regulator in respect of regulated claims management activities."*

<u>No Win No Fee</u>

The apparently simple phrase 'no win no fee' is in fact a complex one to use, particularly in the aftermath of LASPO. The strict rule of the CMR is that it must be used only in accordance with the CAP Help-Note on no win no fee claims. In essence, over the course of three pages The CAP set out what they believe to be non-misleading advertising terms which should be utilised and which should be clear to consumers at the point of any adverts. This author's view is this remains a weak issue across the sector in terms of compliance and ultimately will lead to significant enforcement risks moving forward because if either the SRA or the CMR wanted to address the issue as part of a systematic review then it would be easy to identify and to discipline a number of firms which would struggle to justify their compliance with the CAP Help-Note.

<u>Solicitor Conduct</u>

Principle 8 is a strict prohibition on the CMC acting in anyway which puts any solicitor (read Law Firm) in breach of the rules governing the solicitors' conduct. It mirrors the obligation placed upon you under the Code of Conduct 2011 and which is retained under the proposals from the SRA to amend the Code of Conduct and separate it into a code for firms and a separate code for individuals through the course of 2018 as part of the SRA's regulatory reform.

Practical Tips

1. Know the rules and put the evidential burden on the CMCs (who need this for CMR purposes);

2. Check compliance on an ongoing basis, i.e. document any good or bad points from individual client feedback and look for a pattern; and

3. At least each six months document a review of your CMCs' approach to the rules (create a form to show you have done this!)

Conclusion

As with the earlier part, this guidance is meant to be read in conjunction with the CMCs short and clear Conduct of Authorised Persons Rules 2014. The outline guidance above is designed to flesh out the limitations of the guidance within the Rules themselves and to put some practical context on matters. The key with Conduct of Authorised Persons Rules 2014 is for a law firm to ensure that they have evidence that their CMC is complying and they require the CMC to maintain that evidence and to share it with them on a periodic basis.

CHAPTER FIVE
THE REFERRAL FEE BAN

Introduction

The Legal Aid, Sentencing and Punishment of Offenders Act 2012 (LASPO) contains five relatively short statutory provisions between Section 56 and Section 60 relating to the payment of referral fees in cases involving personal injury and death. Referral fees are only prohibited within the confines of the personal injury and death claims sector.

The successful insurance industry lobbying of successive governments is evidenced most starkly by the decision to focus the referral fee ban purely on claimant personal injury claims. Put bluntly, for defendant matters (read insurance companies), referral fees are not prohibited, and this will not offend the legislation or indeed, the SRA's own guidance. It is only claimant referral fees which are prohibited. In sporting terms it is a mismatch between the Claimant sector which is fragmented and poorly centrally funded and the insurance sector which is well funded with a lobbying function which quickly can focus political influence leading to a lopsided set of restrictions. The statutory rules stemming from LASPO have cut across funding rules changes for CFAs and DBAs and the referral fee ban has jointly as two distinct challenges has led to more and more firms seeking specialist legal advice to comply with increasingly complex legislative and professional obligations separately evolving from the regulators. The referral fee ban reforms have failed in a large part to inhibit the perception of CMC misconduct and in particular cold calling by telephone but the reforms continue to cast a shadow across the future financial viability of the Personal Injury Sector.

It is worth bearing in mind at all times that guidance from regulators can change and the Courts can reinterpret legislation and professional obligations at any time. Nothing is certain in this field. Additionally, this book is not legal advice. My publisher wants me to remind you in each Chapter that you should instruct me to give advice on your specific situation if you need it. The factual circumstances your busi-

ness faces can be assessed and advised on in context which a book simply cannot do.

Section 56 – Rules Against Referral Fees

Under LASPO, the following terms are defined and affect how your firm can operate compliantly with CMCs from 1 April 2013.

Firstly, the prohibitions only apply to Regulated Persons undertaking specified types of Legal Business.

Secondly, there must be a payment or a benefit. In other words, the simple referring of one party to another on a *non-commercial basis* remains permitted, even in the LASPO era.

Thirdly, the "Referral" must be by way of a person providing information to another, which is required to offer the relevant services, and the person providing the information is not the client.

The position can be neatly summarised as the following three questions:

A – Is there a Referral as defined by the Act?

B – Is there a payment?

C – Is the payment for the referral?

The answer to the three questions above must be yes in each case for it to be caught by the LASPO restrictions.

The most common form of exemption from LASPO and the way in which many CMCs and law firms in the personal injury sector have reinvented themselves, is ensuring that there is no referral as defined by the legislation. In simple terms, this means the person providing the information to the law firm must be the client themselves rather than the CMC. For example therefore, it remains perfectly lawful for a CMC to conduct telesales campaigns on data which has been opted in for personal injury claims purposes (see Chapter 8 on the Privacy Electronic Communications Regulations and Data) and to transfer the client on a live call to a personal injury firm and to do so on a no data transferred basis, except by the client ensuring that the client provides their own data in relation to the claim, and that the statutory conditions and definition of what is a referral are demonstratively not met, meaning that the CMC can be paid a fee. Some people have termed this the "recommendation" model. The practical difference is simply that the client is providing their own claims information to the law firm rather than as was historically the case, the CMC collecting that data and then transferring it electronically to the law firm (usually by email or App or a portal).

In practical terms, the people collecting the initial claims data has therefore shifted from the CMC to the law firm, but the information as it comes from the client themselves direct to the law firm is exempt from the definition of a referral.

The SRA's Current Interpretation of Sections 56 to 60 LASPO

One week prior to the referral fee ban coming into place, the SRA published a comprehensive Guidance Note on their interpretation of the legislation. It can be found on the SRA's website under the guidance headed "The Prohibition of Referral Fees in the Legal Aid, Sentencing and Punishment of Offenders Act 2012 (LASPO) Sections 56 to 60" and is dated 25 March 2013.

It sets out the effect of LASPO is that any contract or obligation to pay a referral or any arrangement which is in breach of Section 56 is unenforceable.

Separately, the breaching of the ban is a regulatory breach i.e. to be enforced by the approved legal regulators, rather than a criminal offence. That should not give anyone the impression that it is not a serious issue, as in a judgement published by the Solicitors Disciplinary Tribunal of 2016 involving the *Solicitors Regulation Authority – v – Mark Pearson Ford* Case Number 11272-2006, in the Decision dated 1 November 2016 elected to strike off Mr Ford in part as he put:

"his relationship with users of work ahead of his client's interests".

The basic requirement of clients come first and meeting each and every professional obligation.

How To Engage Claims Management Companies and Comply With the Referral Fee Ban?

The relationship with the CMC must be recorded in writing. A contractual obligation to abide by the Claims Management Regulators (CMR) regime and a warranty in favour of not placing the law firm or the individual solicitor in breach of the SRA's regime will give some comfort.

However, the SRA's current interpretation of matters is focused on firms seeking to verify over and above the contractual relationship between the parties. Warranties and indemnities from contracts alone are not enough; you must evidence their compliance.

All firms are therefore expected not only to conduct due diligence before they enter the referral relationship which may comply with LASPO, but nevertheless, must also comply with the wider obligations under the SRA Rules (see Chapter 3), but also focus on compliance with the PECR and data protection regime (see Chapter 8), and also to conduct an ongoing and sustained audit of the relationship, and monitor the work stemming from the relationship to assess whether or not any issues of concern arise. Some people may think this is excessive! The SRA's view is that it is a risk based model, and once established, the risks should be monitored. This is basic practice in managing risk in other sectors. Put simply, firms should be able to show compliance simply by routine checks.

Practical Steps

The following will assist in demonstrating you are complying with the referral fee ban:

1. Have a written agreement in place with each and every referrer.

2. Have evidence of the due diligence conducted before you enter the relationship with the CMC and monitoring the CMC on an ongoing basis continuing to collate further due diligence (see Chapter 9 for further details on how to do this).

3. Determine whether or not you want to utilise the marketing regime model (see Chapter 6) or the recommendation model (Chapter 7 contains further details).

4. Train your staff with materials that they must complete periodically, recorded and reviewed by the COLP and COFA.

5. Continually apply the statutory definitions of prescribed legal business,"referral" and "regulated person" so that you are constantly holding your sources of work against the referral fee ban criteria. You must ensure their commercial speed/ease solutions do not evolve into a new way of working.

6. Be ready to evidence your compliance at any stage, at short notice, to the SRA. If they asked questions of your business today, how would you demonstrate to them your compliance? When you can answer this question clearly based on evidence you are acting appropriately. Until then, you are running unnecessary risks to your reputation and your professional status.

Conclusion

The approach is simple and initially time consuming, but thereafter, it is a case of:

a) Review;

b) Test; and

c) Evidence the component parts.

For most firms, this can be done in a relatively small amount of time allocated to the task each week. Subsequent chapters will build upon this.

CHAPTER SIX
THE MARKETING MODEL

Introduction

In the run up to the introduction of LASPO on 1 April 2013, a number of dominant models started to emerge. These models were intended to give both law firms and the CMCs they work with the opportunity to continue to work despite the referral fee ban. A number of models were developed by me for clients and I have seen various models developed by other specialists in personal injury or in compliance/regulatory fields.

In this chapter I look at the Marketing Model. It is possible to undertake the Marketing Model in a *compliant* and also in a *non-compliant* manner. The difference? How the scheme works in terms of what is done, and how, against the legislative provisions which were addressed in Chapter 5 (The Referral Fee Ban).

It is worth bearing in mind at all times that guidance from regulators can change and the Courts can reinterpret legislation and professional obligations at any time. Nothing is certain in this field. Additionally, this book is not legal advice. My publisher wants me to remind you in each Chapter that you should instruct me to give advice on your specific situation if you need it. The factual circumstances your business faces can be assessed and advised on in context which a book simply cannot do.

Case Study One – The Marketing Fee Business Model (*Non-Compliant Version*)

CMC Number One Limited is paid a monthly marketing fee by We Don't Care If It Is Compliant Or Not LLP, a firm of solicitors based in a North West market town. CMC Number One Limited publishes adverts in its own name in newspapers and runs a radio campaign and a Facebook campaign in its own name. CMC Number One Limited, when contacted by the potential claimants, sends the details of the potential claims and claimants directly to We Don't Care If It Is Compliant Or Not LLP.

The law firm and the CMC have agreed that they will vary the amounts of monthly payments to reflect the volume of business which is being passed between them. We Don't Care If It Is Compliant Or Not LLP insisted on being able to vary the payments to enable them to manage their cash flow, and also to ensure that they were not paying for leads which were unproductive. CMC Number One Limited provides invoices confirming that their services are for marketing services, and not a specified number of leads as this will, in their view, get around LASPO.

This model is strictly prohibited under LASPO. The passing of details about the potential claim and claimant ensure that here is a referral within the meaning of LASPO. As there is a referral, then inevitably, the payments made are for the referral, and are therefore prohibited.

This model relies upon changing the pre-LASPO terminology of referral fee to a marketing fee. It is akin to calling a mouse an elephant. A mouse is still a mouse and of the rest of the world (in this case, the Claims Management Regulator and the SRA) would call it the same thing. This model should be avoided.

Case Study Two – Marketing Fee Business Model *As Potentially Permitted by LASPO*

Compliant CMC Limited is paid a monthly marketing fee by a firm of solicitors. Compliant CMC Limited advertises in newspapers, on the radio, and on Facebook for potential personal injury claims. Compliant CMC Limited however, does not pass the details directly to the solicitor. Compliant CMC Limited has the potential claimants complete their own information and details into an App which it sends by text message to the potential claimants. The potential claimants therefore complete their own personal details and their own accident details themselves and send this information through the App directly to the solicitor. This means Compliant CMC Limited never holds information that is transferred to the law firm and the only party transferring anything is the client themselves.

The invoices of Compliant CMC Limited confirm that their services are for the marketing of law firms, but that the volume of leads does not affect the services provided or the payment. Payments are the same for each twelve month period and are agreed in advance.

The reason that this model is potentially compliant is that the services are provided irrespective of the volume of claims passing from one entity to the other. Additionally, the statutory definition of referral is not met under LASPO, and therefore, the working method whereby the entirety of the potential claimant's personal details and the claim information is acquired by the law firm direct means the "referral fee ban", as the definition on referral under LASPO expressly excludes situations when an individual provides their own details.

However, the CMR or the SRA could amend or alter their guidance on the application of LASPO at any time and this model whilst it complies with the statutory regime would thus be prohibited – the power to control conduct is with the regulators and therefore you need to be constantly monitoring the regulators perspective and guidance.

<u>Communication of Claim Details – Variation on the LASPO Potentially Compliant Model</u>

The two examples above in the case studies are stark examples of how similar business models can be either compliant or non-compliant by changing who transfers the data.

This is not to say that the working method outlined in the second case study, the potentially compliant one, is the only way forward. Variations on the same theme include the following working methods:

A. if the marketing leads the individual claimants to the solicitors own website, and then they supply their own details online, the definition of referral is, again, excluded under the statutory terms and the model is compliant because the individual is supplying their own details direct to the law firm.

B. The silent hotkey of clients from the CMC to the law firm without exchange of any information is currently permitted. This is probably the most widespread post-LASPO model in the personal injury marketspace. In this manner, the CMC connects the call, but importantly, the client supplies all their details. Again, firms running this model need to be aware that until now the regulators' guidance does not prohibit it but all regulatory rules can be rewritten or amended.

C. The provision by a CMC of access to an App or telephone on which the potential claimants complete their own details i.e. the CMCs phone, or the CMCs tablet or laptop has been used. Strictly speaking under the legislation, the model is compliant. The issue when challenged however, is demonstrating that there is no input into communication transfer from the CMC to the law firm and of course the legislation and regulatory rules give the right to the CMR and SRA to declare it prohibited if they wish. If you can evidence compliance by way of CCTV, by way of recorded telephone calls, or by some other evidential matters, then this can be an option. However, given that it is ambiguous and evidence heavy, it is not for everyone, and is certainly not for the CMCs and law firms who do not have the resources to evidence that it is compliant.

D. Why this model is attractive? Given that the marketing services are purchased for a set fee, and the number of claims received each month by a law firm may vary, the obvious question is why is the marketing model so attractive from a law firm's perspective? The answer put simply, is that it enables the law firm and the CMC to work together, and clearly if the quality of the leads or the number of the leads diminished below a commercially acceptable threshold, then the parties will end their relationship. It is attractive, however, because both the CMC, and the law firm are protected under their respective regulators rules. For CMCs, under the Conduct of Authorised Person Rules 2014, Client Specific Rule 8 prohibits the introduction of a claim to a solicitor if the rules governing solicitors conduct would be breached by that action. In simple terms, the Claims Management Regulator has adopted a rule which requires compliance.

The SRA restriction on this point can be found at Indicative Behaviour 8.6 which prohibits "allowing any other person to conduct publicity for your firm or in-house practice in a way that would breach the Principles".

The approach of both regulators is therefore to place an emphasis on the law firm being compliant, but also ensuring that no act would undermine the rules of conduct used by the other.

Just Plain Silly Approaches

Suggestions were made prior to the introduction of LASPO that firms would seek to share damages or share legal fees with CMCs to get around LASPO. This is just plain silly because LASPO strictly prohibits payment in any form, whether that is before the referral, or afterwards.

It is also just plain silly not to check at least quarterly, and ideally monthly, a portion of the work undertaken by a CMC on your firm's behalf. You are not expected to watch each and every step, but you are expected to have an awareness of what is being done in your name. If you spot something which is untoward being undertaken on behalf of your firm and you do not do something about it, then the SRA's enforcement approach suggests that they will impose a sanction on you either by agreement using a Regulatory Settlement Agreement (which usually includes a fine and prohibitions on future actions), or in more serious cases, by referral to the Solicitors Disciplinary Tribunal.

Ensuring that you get expert advice on your model and reviewing your model periodically is essential as it is difficult if not impossible to assess the risks yourself without seeing how the SRA and CMR are auditing firms at that time. Your model, whatever you finally choose it to be, should be reviewed periodically so that an objective view of the working methods is taken.

Conclusion

The Marketing Model was, for a period of time, the dominant model that emerged after the introduction of LASPO. The position has become more balanced with the recommendation model now, but nevertheless, it remains the most popular LASPO era model, and it has much to commend it from a law firm's perspective in terms of offering the opportunity to limit the acquisition costs of clients, and to clearly demonstrate efforts to ensure compliance with the LASPO restrictions on referrals.

CHAPTER SEVEN
THE RECOMMENDATION MODEL

Introduction

This chapter is intended to be read in conjunction with chapters 5 & 6 regarding the referral fee bank and marketing model as firms need to choose what works for them commercially and demonstrate that it complies with their statutory obligations and their separate but just as vital professional obligations.

It is worth bearing in mind at all times that guidance from regulators can change and the Courts can reinterpret legislation and professional obligations at any time. Nothing is certain in this field. Additionally, this book is not legal advice. My publisher wants me to remind you in each Chapter that you should instruct me to give advice on your specific situation if you need it. The factual circumstances your business faces can be assessed and advised on in context which a book simply cannot do.

Recommendation, a referral fee in disguise?

In the immediate aftermath after the introduction of LASPO we saw a number of law firms and CMCs using a referral fee agreement which had effectively tippexed out the word referral and had replaced it with recommendation. The suggestion was that this in itself, by changing the wording, was enough. It was of course an absurd position adopted by desperate business owners trying to keep their businesses afloat in the aftermath of seismic regulatory change.

The recommendation model which has emerged since however is slightly more sophisticated in that it takes advantage of an opportunity provided by section 56 of LASPO. There is no uniform way of operating the model and therefore, as in chapter 6 regarding the marketing model, two case studies are given to explain the position.

Case study one – the recommendation model (non-compliant version)

Who Cares About Compliance Limited, a CMC authorised by the CMR, conducts telesales on behalf of a panel of law firms and is based in a North West city suburb. Who Cares About Compliance Limited obtains data and marketing lists from third parties who have conducted surveys and have, using online social media platforms, procured from individuals their name, email addresses and telephone number. Who Cares About Compliance Limited calls those contacts to ask them if they have been involved in a road traffic accident or other personal injury matter and then sends the details to each of its law firm panel members on a rota basis. It says in each email it sends to the law firm panel members,

> *"This is a recommendation to the individual to use your firm. You will need to pay us a recommendation fee of £500 plus VAT if you take the client on. If you reject the client you will need to tell us and we will reallocate them to another of our panel".*

From Chapter 5 you will recall the guidance that the position regarding compliance can be neatly summarised as the following three questions:

A – Is there a Referral as defined by the Act?

B – Is there a payment?

C – Is the payment <u>for</u> the referral?

The model outlined above is using these simple questions strictly prohibited under LASPO. Firstly, the passing of the client's details about the potential claim and claimant ensure there is a referral within the meaning of LASPO. As there is a referral, then inevitably, the payments proposed are made for the referral and it is strictly prohibited. It is cold calling because the consumers have not expressly opted in to receive calls about their potential claims and/or legal services.

Additionally, from a compliance perspective, the cold calling of individuals about whether or not they have had an accident is strictly prohibited.

As with the example in the previous chapter, it is akin to calling a mouse an elephant. A mouse is still a mouse unless the rest of the world calls it something else. This model should be avoided.

<u>Case study two – the recommendation model (as potentially permitted)</u>

Compliance CMC Limited obtains opted in data lists for those that have been involved in road traffic accidents and workplace accidents from a data house authorised and regulated by the ICO and the CMR (as they are selling accident data it needs to be both). The source of the opt-in is evidenced and available to Compliance CMC Limited, as required by CMR, and to law firms who are on Compliance CMC Limited's law firm panel. When clients confirm they would like recommendation on to a law firm, a silent hot key transfer occurs meaning that no data has passed from Compliance CMC Limited to the law firm. The law firm then takes the potential claimant's personal details and details about the accident. Having come through a dedicated telephone line, and having been accepted, the law firm pays Compliance CMC Limited a fee of £500 plus VAT for the recommendation.

The invoices of Compliance CMC Limited confirm that the recommendation was made to the claimant and that they were silently hot keyed through to provide their own information in order to demonstrate LASPO compliance. Payments therefore are on a case by case basis as was the position with the referral fees which were ultimately banned by LASPO, but the method of achieving this complies with section 56 of LASPO.

The reason that this model is potentially compliant is because the services are provided only after the client has provided their own data. In effect, what this means is there is no data transfer between the CMC and the law firm because of the use of silent hot key transfers. It relies entirely on the statutory definition of a referral not being met under LASPO statutory provisions and therefore, is a working method whereby LASPO is not engaged. The working methods are key to compliance hence a general "this method works" is difficult to achieve as because as any time the SRA and CMR could introduce revised guidance which would undermine the models in use by firms.

Practical Tips

1. Obtain and verify the opt-in to show it is for the client's personal opt-in and not a generic opt-in;
2. Check three percent of each data set you purchase; and
3. Investigate any client's claim of being cold called so you can show this did not occur.

Conclusion

At first the recommendation model can seem to be a referral, but it is not a referral within the meaning of LASPO if the client rather than a third party (i.e. a CMC) provides that data. This excludes the model from the LASPO restricted conduct. However the CMR and the SRA upon client audits can and do challenge the working methods and firms must be prepared to demonstrate compliance upon audit and investigation. When this model first appeared the auditors of the SRA and SMR struggled with the model given it resembled the now prohibited referral fee model. However, once they understood that the legislation did not become engaged the regulators started to ask different questions to look at wider compliance and to assess the law firms or CMCs working methods.

In my view, it is a model which, ultimately, both regulators and parliamentarians will look to address in the future not least as it circumvents the intended prohibitions introduced by LASPO using a very similar set of working methods, which probably were not foreseen by Parliament when the restrictions were drafted. Therefore inevitably I expect further action to reduce CMC activity and to limit claims. My instinct is the regulators will conclude that changing professional obligations is the key to achieving their statutory obligations under section 1 of the LSA 2007 regarding consumer protection and maintenance of trust in the legal services and not a law firms natural more commercially focused aim of making a profit from helping clients.

The onus to demonstrate compliance is on the law firm and the CMC to each regulator. The practical tips above highlight the evidence needed.

CHAPTER EIGHT
PRIVACY AND ELECTRONIC COMMUNICATIONS REGULATION (DIRECT MARKETING BITES)

Introduction

Law firms and Claims Management Companies (CMCs) often think they need to focus on the Data Protection Act 1998 and how they deal with data and sharing information but in reality for the majority of these businesses the Privacy and Electronic Communications (EC Directive) Regulations 2003 (known as PECR) is the first hurdle to jump before addressing the data protection issues.

The purpose of the PECR is to regulate specified activities linked to data protection and privacy. The PECR sits alongside the more widely known about DPA legislation to compliment the protections given to us all about our data and its use.

The PECR covers:

1. **Marketing by any electronic means**, including: marketing calls (telesales and call Centres), text message , email and for the dinosaurs amongst us faxes (apparently they still exist);

2. The **use of "Cookies"** that track information about website usage. Cookies are perhaps best known for resulting in those "Privacy Notice" or "Cookie Consent" pop ups we are all familiar with when browsing the internet;

3. **Security of public electronic communications services**. This is really about network providers and their security for the underlying telecoms and internet systems;

4. **Privacy of customers** using communications networks or services as regards traffic and location data, itemised billing, line

identification services (e.g. caller ID and call return), and directory listings.

You will immediately appreciate that the latter two circumstances lie far outside the scope of this book. The first two are however highly relevant and we will examine their relevance in some depth in this chapter.

It is worth bearing in mind at all times that guidance from regulators can change and the Courts can reinterpret legislation and professional obligations at any time. Nothing is certain in this field. Additionally, this book is not legal advice. My publisher wants me to remind you in each Chapter that you should instruct me to give advice on your specific situation if you need it. The factual circumstances your business faces can be assessed and advised on in context which a book simply cannot do.

What about Brexit and the PECR?

The United Kingdom has, following the referendum held on the 23rd June 2016, decided to leave the European Union. Most days since then a client or potential client has enquired something along the lines of:

When we will be free of all this data protection mess?

The brutal reality is the bits that bite law firms and that CMCs get investigated on (telesales data and loss of data) are here to stay. The PECR may stem from European Directive 2002/58/EC and may contain in the UK version title "EC Directive" but the regulations are already enshrined in the United Kingdom's own legislation (Scotland, Wales and Northern Ireland may have devolved administrations with distinct agendas but the position is unlikely to change as limiting consumers' privacy to promote marketing options is unlikely to be high on any political agenda).

General Data Protection Regulation (GDPR)

On the 25th May 2018 the UK's data protection regime will undergo a seismic change with the introduction of the GDPR which will amend the data protection regime and will amend or repeal elements of the DPA.

The guidance on the GDPR for all organisations, not just CMCs and law firms is an ever changing and developing area and is outside the scope of this book which deals with the current position. In future editions I hope to cover the GDPR once the position is clear from the regulators' perspective.

Does the PECR apply to me?

If you are marketing personal injury legal services then the PECR will apply to you if you market:

- by telephone (this way the majority of CMCs are caught);
- by email (including law firm newsletters to consumers or by CMC following "opt-in" by individuals/consumers;
- by text message (to individual/consumers);
- by sending faxes (to individuals/consumers)
- using cookies on your law firms or CMC website.

PECR is pervasive and therefore if you are marketing using telesales or electronic (database) marketing your business will need to consider the implications for your business.

<u>Telesales and Law Firms</u>

For law firms, marketing by telesales directly is expressly prohibited under the SRA Code of Conduct 2011 by way of the following mandatory outcome:

> *"O (8.3) you do not make unsolicited approaches in person or by telephone to members of the public in order to publicise your firm or in-house practice or another business;"*[1]

Telesales should be avoided by law firms dealing with consumers therefore. By contrast non-personal injury law firms undertaking commercial work can use telesales as they are calling businesses and not consumers. The position may appear unfair and even anti-competitive to some but consumers' interests have been prioritised in terms of protection, by contrast businesses can look after themselves seems to be the underlying ethos.

A CMC can make telesales calls only with the client's or potential client's consent. This is exactly the same as for law firms under the Code of Conduct 2011.

CMCs are not bound by the Code of Conduct 2011 directly as their regulation stems from different sources. However the CMR does restrict telesales by an obligation that any such marketing shall be in accordance with the DMA's Code and any related guidance issued by the DMA. Therefore in reality CMCs are regulated by:

1. The CMR regime;
2. The ICO for data usage and breaches;
3. The DMA Codes.

The indirect aspect of the Code of Conduct 2011 to CMCs is this: if law firms accept work obtained in breach of the Code of Conduct 2011 then the law firm is open to disciplinary sanction. Additionally, the Conduct of Authorised Persons Rules 2014, at Client Specific Rule 8 prohibits marketing which places a solicitor in breach of the SRA rules.

It does not seem fair that the personal injury market is regulated distinctly from the rest of legal services and in such a fragmented way.

1 See chapter on SRA Regulation if to develop your understand the mandatory outcomes approach of the SRA

However the prevalence of cold calling claims businesses means the sector has been targeted for regulation as it continues to battle with the actions of a minority of CMCs.

PECR and the Data Protection Act 1998

The DPA continues to apply at all times, the PECR simply compliments the DPA but the regime introduced by PECR focuses on the detailed privacy implications of electronic communications which inevitably is a developing and emerging area alongside emerging technologies. For instance, in 2003 email marketing was still relatively in its infancy as mass access web based emails were introduced the 1990s with Hotmail (now Outlook.com) launching in 1996. Email rapidly emerged and by 2003 was widespread in many workplaces. However when the PECR were introduced social media was yet to be a widespread concept. The regulations were intended to evolve with new forms of electronic communications as the technologies developed.

The relationship of the PECR with the DPA is expressly dealt with within the regulations:

> ***"Relationship between these Regulations and the Data Protection Act 1998***
>
> *4. Nothing in these Regulations shall relieve a person of his obligations under the Data Protection Act 1998 in relation to the processing of personal data."*[2]

One of the major challenges of compliance for law firms and the CMCs they work with is therefore evidencing systematically the compliance with both the DPA and PECR. A theme throughout this book that we will return time and time again is that compliance is not a one-off process but a continuous process which once commenced has to be repeated time and time again. The PECR, for the reasons set out in the rest of the chapter, is the starkest example of this.

---

2 Regulation 4 PECR 2003

Organisational Issues

The PECR applies to all electronic communications so the existence of personal data for marketing is not essential as the PECR still applies. The DPA by contrast requires personal data to take effect. Hence the PECR has a wider application which can catch out the unaware leading to enforcement action if organisations focus on the DPA and fail to address the PECR.

Case Study – Don't Rely On Others

In 2016 the ICO published details of a fine and enforcement notice imposed on Intelligent Lending trading as Ocean Finance who was fined £130,000 for sending spam text messages to consumers offering services when they believed they had the consent of the recipients.

This case study is a good example of the strict nature of the PECR regime.

According to the ICO's press release 28th September 2016 Intelligent Lending was assured by the data company who supplied the data that the data was opted-in data and the company could send the texts. They failed to check the consent was valid for their intended purposes and incurred a large fine and have a prohibition on sending any other text messages for marketing purposes in the future.

Law firms can be held liable for CMC activities in the same manner. Law firms need to evidence the CMCs compliance and should seek verifiable evidence of the compliance of each component party (data supplier, CMC and law firms).

The key to compliance with the PECR is therefore:

1. Check at the outset of the trading relationship if the consent is sufficient for PECR purposes;

2. Check a sufficient percentage to ensure you can evidence compliance;

3. Check a percentage of every data set and every month;

4. Retain records of the above. For law firms retaining the records for 6 years is appropriate given the Legal Ombudsman scheme time limit.

Telephone Marketing

When law firms or CMCs are conducting telephone marketing they must conduct some preliminary checks. These are:

1. The caller's number must displayed;

2. The callers must not make marketing calls to any number listed on the Telephone Preference Service (TPS) or Corporate TPS (CTPS), unless that individual has specifically consented to calls from that organisation;

3. The callers can only call a number if it is not listed on the TPS or CTPS.

In practical terms therefore organisations need to screen call lists against the TPS and CTPS lists which as a minimum should be updated every 28 days. The TPS offer this service themselves (for a charge) or many data houses include such a service. If you rely on the data house or commercial partner the key thing to ask is:

How do we evidence this has been done?

The answer is you need proof that numbers have been suppressed and many CMCs hold a file of such numbers against their data list. Law firms being told this has been done should ask to see the suppression list periodically and screen the suppressed numbers against the clients introduced (any IT technician should be able to do this if you cannot using an Excel spreadsheet).

Consent – Opt In - Evidence is not optional

If the consent to receive marketing messages is not explicit then law firms risk the CMCs undertaking marketing on their behalf which is unlawful and of course this is a potential professional disciplinary offence under the Code of Conduct 2011 and the mandatory Outcome 8.3 which states:

> *"O (8.3) you do not make unsolicited approaches in person or by telephone to members of the public in order to publicise your firm or in-house practice or another business;"*

The key to this professional obligation being that unless the consent is adequate then the approach is unsolicited and prohibited (in respect of consumer law areas such as personal injury). The fact that the CMC does the work is not a defence because of Indicative Behavior obligations arising:

> *"IB (8.6) allowing any other person to conduct publicity for your firm or in-house practice in a way that would breach the Principles;"*

In respect of clients I have acted for under SRA investigation the fact that a third party has conducted tasks is helpful when the law firm have picked the issue up themselves and taken steps to terminate the contractual relationship. In other words it helps that it is a third party but it does not exonerate the firm (or individual solicitors).

The opt-in or consent must be clear and unambiguous for the type of legal service being offered. For personal injury firms this is therefore "a claim for personal injury" or a similar wording. A general opt-in is insufficient.

The CMR Bulletin 26 October 2015 indicates the high threshold for law firms and CMCs. In summary, no CMC (and by default law firm) can contact a consumer by telephone unless:

a) they have explicitly agreed to be contacted about making a claim;

b) the potential claimant's contact details were not obtained as a result of an unsolicited approach;

c) both of the above criteria must be met prior to any telesales actives.

This applies to all firms of electronic marketing including email, telesales by live call and telesales by automated message.

What are the rules on using automated messages?

Under Regulation 19 the regime for the use of automatic calls is very strict, deliberately so. The restrictions apply to any call made by an automated dialing system that plays a recorded message to the person receiving the call.

CMCs who use this technique should be viewed very sceptically by law firms as it is highly unlikely that their use is appropriate for leads into a law firm. The SRA Handbook 2011 states:

> *"Principle 6: [you] behave in a way that maintains the trust the public places in you and in the provision of legal services;"*

And in Chapter 8 of the Code of Conduct 2011:

> *"IB (8.6) allowing any other person to conduct publicity for your firm or in-house practice in a way that would breach the Principles;"*

The maintenance of public confidence in the legal profession is unlikely to be maintained by automated call usage and hence the SRA will always have an enforcement option against law firms which allows their CMCs to market them in such a manner.

The PECR requires under Regulation 19 that the receiver of the call has expressly consented to receive such messages from the organisation making the call. A general consent to receive marketing is not sufficient it must be specific to the organisation involved and the purpose of the communication. So, to the consent opt-in above at (a) to (c), add:

d) the potential claimant has expressly consented to receive automated messages.

These strict restrictions and the SRA Handbook obligations mean I shall not focus further on this type of marketing as it is so unsuited to law firms and CMCs and the options to undertake it lawfully and within the regulations are too narrowly drawn for it to have general effect.

What are the rules on making live calls?

Under Regulation 21 direct marketing businesses must not make unsolicited live calls to:

1. anyone who has said previously they don't want their calls; or
2. any number registered with the TPS or CTPS (this applies unless the person has specifically consented to the calls – even if they are an existing customer so it's a harsh regime).

The wider regime imposes further obligations. As a minimum direct marketing businesses must always:

1. say who is calling, for example "This is ABC Limited calling....";
2. show a caller ID number to be displayed to the person receiving the call;
3. provide a contact address or freephone number to enable those receiving the calls to opt-out (this duty arising from ICO Guidance[3] and not regulation 21)

These simple steps will keep your reputation as a law firm safe and are easily verifiable by law firms working with CMCs. Ask the clients potentially referred if these obligations were met.

---

3 See Information Commissioners Office Direct marketing 20160519 Version: 2.2

The CMR publishes an enforcement bulletin each quarter looking at the trends and for 2016 and the last quarter (October to December 2016) for which information is available at the time of writing the following trends emerge:

- issued financial penalties for failing to conduct sufficient due diligence on the leads generating sources;
- audited CMCs undertaking PECR compliance and issuing comprehensive written advice
- warnings issued to CMCs for non-compliant direct marketing;
- agreed a written undertaking with a CMC for an email campaign without ensuring appropriate consent was obtained;
- commenced a series of investigations into CMCs for potential and alleged breaches of PECR rules (focusing on telephone, text and email marketing);
- conducted hundreds of visits of previously authorised CMCs to ensure that they were not undertaking unauthorised activities having ceased to be authorised;
- prosecuted individuals behind unauthorised CMCs, who buy and sell stolen or fraudulent accident data and worked with specialist police investigation teams focusing on linked areas (fraudulent claims, organised crime groups and with other regulators).

The key thing for law firms and CMCs making telephone calls is ensuring the habits of the firm making such calls are good ones. The following covers the basic issues:

1. conduct due diligence on the CMCs your law firm intends to contract with;

2. conduct due diligence on the consent (opt-in) for the type of direct marketing being undertaken under the PECR;
3. train all staff on what they can and cannot say during telesales calls;
4. use a script to prevent sales misconduct;
5. monitor the calls and listen to any call recordings;
6. ensure the CMCs address any failings and keep records of the CMCs actions.

In other chapters other points are developed and introduced.

Fax Marketing – The Dinosaur Option

In my day-to-day practice of advising clients fax marketing has not arisen as a key source of marketing in the personal injury or financial services sectors for many years. I suspect like the dinosaurs this is extinct but for completeness of assessing the PECR here is what you need to know if you are intent on fax marketing.

Regulation 20 of PECR applies to marketing by fax.

Briefly, your CMCs must not send marketing faxes to:

- individuals unless they have consented to your faxes (this including sole traders and in limited circumstances some partnerships); or
- a company or other corporate body that has told you they do not want your faxes; or
- any number registered with the Fax Preference Service, unless the person has specifically consented to your faxes.

All marketing faxes must include your name and a contact address or freephone number to enable the recipient to get themselves removed from your mailing list.

Electronic mail marketing (aka email, texts and social media)

In 2003 when the PECR were introduced as outlined earlier in this chapter it was clear that technologies were going to develop. The rules apply equally to the established technologies such as text messages as to online marketing (sometimes called viral marketing) when data is used to target by way of messages to individuals.

PECR Regulation 22 guides CMCs that they must not send electronic mail marketing to individuals, unless:

- they have specifically consented to electronic mail from the party sending the marketing messages (called the sender under Regulation 22); or
- the messages are to an existing customer who bought (or negotiated to buy) a similar product or service from you in the past, and you gave them a way to opt in or out when you first collected their details and in every message you have sent.

You must identify your business, and you must provide a valid contact address so they can opt-out or unsubscribe at any time of their choosing. The effects of Regulation 22 are that the dominant method of "opt-in" should be consent to receive marketing from the party sending the messages. For law firms therefore contracting with CMCs to obtain new clients for their business it is simple to check the consent if electronic mail marketing is used (email, text messages and direct messages on social media) by checking that the consent says:

"I consent to receive marketing notifications from ABC Limited about personal injury claims"

Failure to obtain a specific enough opt-in risks the CMR applying the "Client Specific Rule" regime and commencing an investigation and/or enforcement action:

> *"4. Cold calling in person is prohibited. Any marketing by telephone, email, fax or text shall be in accordance with the Direct Marketing Association's Code and any related guidance issued by the Direct Marketing Association."*[4]

Law firms and CMCs should, to work compliantly, relentlessly focus on the specific nature of the consent to receive messages about personal injury matters and from the sender in question. The CMR's onerous position on consent can be summarised as follows:

a) the consumer must have explicitly agreed to be contacted about making a claim; and

b) the consumers contact details were not originally obtained as a result of an unsolicited approach, in person or by telephone by any party (the CMC or a third party).[5]

The consent must be unambiguous for personal injury marketing therefore due to the DPA, PECR, CMR and SRA obligations on CMCs and Solicitors.

Buying a marketing list

The sale of databases and marketing lists is big business and is commonplace. However, the risks are high as CMCs need to be able to demonstrate to the CMR (and therefore law firms need to be able to evidence) that the source of data was not prohibited. When buying a database this can be difficult.

---

4 Conduct of Authorised Persons Rules 2014 Effective from 1 October 2014

5 Full details are contained in the Claims Management Regulators Bulleting 26 (October 2015) which can accesses online https://www.gov.uk/government/publications/cmr-bulletin-26/cmr-bulletin-26#cold-calling-for-personal-injury-claims---reminder

If you wish to buy a list the following points may assist:

1. Is the seller a reputable company? You can show this by
   a. their ICO registration;
   b. the absence of enforcement actions against them;
   c. a review of the company's online feedback – if negative avoid them as the regulator will ask if you have put profit ahead of compliance;
   d. a review of the directors interests at Companies House;
   e. contractual terms to protect your law firm and the consumers involved;
   f. verifying a sample of the consent opt-in and screening the list against the TPS list yourself).
2. What is the stated source of the consent/opt-in and what evidence of this is available?
3. Buying a smaller sample list initially and then buying more data after this has been shown to be lawfully obtained;
4. Following the ICO's guidance on buying lists (and for law firms their COLP should be recording why they have considered it appropriate to buy a list or from a CMC that has).

Who cares if we breach PECR?

Consumers care greatly about their privacy and the recent trend for serious enforcement fines from the ICO shows this.

The ICO has a number of enforcement options. These are:

- Criminal prosecution of the individuals behind unlawful direct marketing (but this is limited to offences under the Data Protection Act 1998;

- Issuing a Civil Enforcement Notice against the company of up to £500,000;
- Issuing a "Stop Now" notice to individuals and organisations to restrict what they are permitted to do (and making any breaches a criminal offence);
- Applying to the Court for an order under section 213 of the Enterprise Act 2002 requiring a person to cease conduct harmful to consumers.

The fines tend to get the publicity but having advised a number of marketing businesses who have found themselves under siege from the ICO and linked bodies such a Police and Trading Standards the disruption to the business is onerous. The ICO's powers are deliberately wide and designed to disrupt.

For law firms any action by the ICO would almost certainly lead to an SRA investigation and thus potentially to additional sanction.

For CMCs the CMR may use its wide powers to investigate and remove a CMCs authorisation.

It is all fairly draconian and disruptive. If you find yourself on the end of such action a general book such as this is inadequate. You need expert legal advice personalised to your position.

PECR Conclusion

Privacy for consumers is the key to the PECR compliance in respect of the direct marketing issues. Check that what you are doing is allowed against the PECR and your Code of Conduct.

Evidence what you are doing against the regulations (10% is a good starting point with a new supplier).

Think about the evidence required to show compliance at each stage and record your reasons for collecting it (ideally through your COLP in your Risk Register).

If in any doubt, do not carry on. Suspend until you have evidence of compliance that you are comfortable explaining and showing to the SRA (and for CMCs to the CMR)

Use the checklists at the end of this book to help you manage the issues arising from this chapter.

CHAPTER NINE
DUE DILIGENCE EXPECTATIONS

Introduction

The term due diligence is widely used across the legal sector, but of course means different things in different contexts. In the context of a personal injury law firm looking to enter into a relationship with a CMC or multiple CMCs, there are three key regulatory bodies who would expect an effective understanding of each party's risks and responsibilities. The purpose of the due diligence in this context is to ensure that the risks are identified, and thereafter can be managed.

When risks are managed, they may not be eliminated, and in the next chapter we will also look at the audit function for compliance teams within law firms. Firstly however, in this chapter we will look at the expectations of each of the regulators.

It is worth bearing in mind at all times that guidance from regulators can change and the Courts can reinterpret legislation and professional obligations at any time. Nothing is certain in this field. Additionally, this book is not legal advice. My publisher wants me to remind you in each Chapter that you should instruct me to give advice on your specific situation if you need it. The factual circumstances your business faces can be assessed and advised on in context which a book simply cannot do.

Who Cares About Marketing of Personal Injury Claims?

From the other chapters in this book, you will have already identified that there are three key regulators to be satisfied. Firstly, the SRA, as the law firms' primary regulator will want to be satisfied that the law firm is not endangering the best interests of each client.

Secondly, the ICO, which has responsibility for requirements introduced by the DPA and PECR, dealt with in other chapters earlier.

The third and almost, to a degree, least relevant, would be the CMR, until of course the CMR takes an investigation forward to enforcement action, when the CMR will be suddenly a higher priority in terms of their thinking, on a CMC.

The SRA Agenda

The SRA Agenda in relation to due diligence is based around three Principles, and, arguably, two Mandatory Outcomes.

Principle 3 requires that the law firm shall not "allow your independence to be compromised".

In practical terms, this means that a CMC cannot, under any circumstances, influence the advice that may be given to a client. If you are engaging with CMCs therefore, you need to be able to evidence that any risk of a perception that your firm's independent advice to each and every client may have been compromised by, for example, a financial relationship between the CMC and the law firm, will not be impinged.

Principle 4 requires that the law firm shall "act in the best interests of each client" on each and every occasion and without exception. In other words, the client's interests prevail over both the law firm's and the CMCs. When dealing with large numbers of claimants, and when there is an ongoing commercial relationship, how would you demonstrate, if required to, that the interests of each client are being served?

Principle 6 requires law firms to "behave in a way that maintains the trust the public places in you and in the provision of legal services". In other words, you must be able to demonstrate through your due diligence that the public can trust the relationship you have with third parties, including CMCs, and others (car hire businesses or medical agencies).

In terms of the Mandatory Outcomes, Outcome 4.1 requires that you "keep the affairs of clients confidential, unless disclosure is required or permitted by law, or the client consents".

The law firm must also have effective systems and controls in place to enable them to identify the risks of client confidentiality and to mitigate those risks (Outcome 4.5).

In terms of the relationship with CMCs therefore, the checklists provided in later chapters are highly relevant. They are how you can start to build evidence of the due diligence undertaken.

As an overview, here are some factors to consider.

Who Are You Dealing With?

Are you dealing with a CMC which is registered with the CMR? Do you have evidence of that registration and all the trading names being used?

Do you know who the directors and shadow directors of the business are? Are you able to prove their identities and check their reputations online?

Have you obtained a credit report into the company and/or its directors to verify that they are financially secure and will not be unduly influenced by financial pressures?

Systems and Processes

What systems and processes do your CMCs have in place? How could you identify what training their staff has had?

In terms of electronic or telephone equipment, how do you know that it is being utilised in accordance with the requirements of PECR and that the clients have consented to be contacted?

Before You Enter Into A Relationship With A CMC

You should be able to investigate and document who you are dealing with and how they deal with the issues outlined above and within questionnaires.

Your due diligence should be obtained and dated to evidence the date at which it was secured.

You should also be revisiting the due diligence to see whether or not anything has changed. Are the directors different? Has the online reputation of the CMC changed? Has the CMR taken disciplinary action? Has the registration with the ICO lapsed? The point made by the checklists in the later chapters for your use, and here, is that due diligence in relation to CMCs is not a one off. It must be systematic and ongoing. The due diligence process, once you decide to work with a CMC therefore, never ceases.

The Expectations of The Information Commissioner's Office

The ICO publishes a number of Data Protection self-assessment toolkits. The use of these checklists provides good evidence of what you are doing and what your suppliers are doing in relation to DPA and PECR.

If a CMC is doing work on your behalf, you should ask them to complete the self-assessments and to provide you with a copy of the evidence supporting their processes.

The ICO's processes in terms of the checklist is located at https://ico.org.uk/for-organisations/resources-and-support/data-protection-self-assessment-toolkit/. The toolkits provide the following guidance:

- Data Protection insurance for first time users assessing compliance with the DPA;
- Getting ready for the GDPR;
- Information security – assessing compliance with information security policies and risks;
- Direct marketing;

- Records management, including record creation, storage and disposal;
- Data sharing and subject access.

These self-assessment toolkits are designed to support and evidence your compliance from an ICO perspective. They are invaluable as well from an SRA perspective. Your Compliance Team should be familiar with them, and should be asking your CMCs to familiarise themselves with the provision of these assessments on a periodic basis (depending upon the size of your organisation and the link, that could be from everything every quarter to annually).

Claims Management Regulator

The CMR expects you to make rigorous checks to satisfy yourself that the CMC obtained the personal data fairly and lawfully. This means that your CMCs must be able to demonstrate this when asked. Whilst the following chapter deals with audit, if they cannot provide that information to you, how would they provide it to their regulator, the CMR?

As a minimum, CMCs must check how and when consent to receive marketing regarding the services was obtained, and what the customer was told.

Obtaining copies of the consent itself is key. If your CMC is buying a list of 100,000 numbers to call on a telesales operation, they should be seeking sufficient evidence to know how that consent was obtained and what the consumer was told.

Practical Tips

1. Due diligence should be an ongoing process and should occur before entering into a commercial relationship, and periodically thereafter to reflect the risks and the type of work you under-

take. Keeping a log of your decision as to how frequently and how often you will repeat is key.

2. Checking the organisations and the individuals you are dealing with in terms of their online reputation is key. These logs should be retained to be evidenced if the need ever arises.

3. CMCs which are unable to provide evidence of their own compliance as a matter of routine should be avoided. The CMR expects them to be able to audit and provide this, so if you are asking for it and they do not have it, then you know they are a high risk CMC.

CHAPTER TEN
AUDIT

Introduction

To quote the Tom Cruise movie Jerry Maguire *"Show me the money"*, when the SRA or CMR look into the relationship between a law firm and CMC they will inevitably look for the money and what the money is being spent on and why. This is not so much 'show me the money', as 'show me the evidence of compliance'.

The word audit has many different meanings, its most common form being a financial audit conducted by qualified accountants known as auditors, but also the file review process within law firms. In this context, audit means the acquisition of evidence through systems and processes which enable you to demonstrate to the SRA that your firm is operating in a compliant manner.

Why Does This Matter?

There is no express requirement for the carrying out of file audits contained in the SRA Code of Conduct 2011, or indeed, the forthcoming, currently in draft so subject to potential amendments, SRA Code of Conduct [2018]. Nevertheless, in the absence of an express requirement, it is fairly obvious that audits to manage risk within the practice, including the risks posed by CMCs, are an essential component of the process of managing a law firm's risk.

Looking at the SRA Authorisation Rules 2011, which are, as you will recall from the section on the SRA's compliance regime, the rules which govern the authorisation of the firm, these specifically guide at Authorisation Rule 8.2(a) (i) as follows:

> ***"Suitable arrangements For Compliance***
>
> a) *An authorised body must at all times have suitable arrangements in place to ensure that:*

i) *The body, its managers and employees comply with the SRA's regulatory arrangements as they apply to them, as required under Section 176 of the Legal Services Act and Rule 8.1 above; and*

ii) *The body and its managers and employees who are authorised persons maintain the professional principles."*

The very clear steer, albeit hidden in the depths of the Authorisation Rules, to firms is that they must be able to demonstrate compliance. In terms of CMCs, this demonstration of compliance is impossible, I suggest, without some form of review which gathers and retains evidence for future inspection. If you are currently working with CMCs, ask yourself:

a) If the SRA arrived this morning at your firm, what evidence would you be able to provide to them to demonstrate that you have assessed the threat posed to your compliance by the CMC?

b) What evidence will you be able to provide that demonstrates that, for example, a CMC undertaking telesales to opted in customers actually has an effective opt-in?

If you cannot demonstrate this, then, of course, you risk prosecution under the DPA, PECR and, of course, professional sanction under the SRA regime.

Like the rest of the Handbook, the Authorisation Rules contain, occasional useful guidance notes imbedded within the documentation. The guidance note to Rule 8.2 reads as follows:

*"**Rule 8.2** deals with the need for law firms to have suitable arrangements for compliance (see also Chapter 7 of the SRA Code of Conduct (Management of your Business)). What needs to be covered by a firm's compliance plan will depend upon factors such as the size and nature of the firm, the work, and specific areas of risk. Firms will need to analyse the effectiveness of their compliance arrangements before applying for authorisation, and monitor effectiveness on an ongoing basis once authorised."*

The final sentence I must particularly draw your attention to. The ability to demonstrate compliance applies both before you apply for authorisation (if you are starting a firm), and on an ongoing basis. It is a never-ending obligation. Firms which conduct the due diligence suggested in the checklists within Chapter 12 will note that they, in their precedent form, contain guidance to conduct them on a periodic basis, and for some firms that period may be more frequently than the precedent suggests, and for others, additional questions will arise. Put bluntly therefore, in relation to auditing, you need to demonstrate compliance with the rest of the material contained in this book, and in the SRA Handbook 2011 more generally.

What Should You Audit?

The short answer is everything. The need to audit will of course vary depending upon the type of CMC that you are working with in terms of what type of marketing they undertake on your behalf. If they are engaged in telesales, then the focus will be on ensuring that cold calling is avoided and that the potential clients have opted in to receive such calls. In contrast, if it is web-based advertising, the audit focus will be on ensuring that the advertising is not misleading and does not offend the CAP Code of Practice. When drawing up a list of audit areas, the following general guidance may be of use. The likely key elements of any audit programme include:

a) Assessing and recording whether or not the contract for the provision of CMC services covers all of the marketing methods utilised by the CMC?;

b) Confirming that the contractual arrangements with the CMC have been signed by both parties;

c) Ensuring that the initial call-handling staff are aware and understand the requirements of the compliance regime and are alerted as to what matters they should bring towards the attention of their supervisor/COLP;

d) Identify any potential compliance failings and investigate these;

e) Reviewing, by way of a GAP analysis, the procedures which are being utilised in respect of sharing of information, and ensuring that an express client consent to the sharing of any information from the law firm with any third parties is in place;

f) Ensuring that any issues and investigations are brought to the attention of the COLP, COFA, Authorised Managers (those persons who owe a duty of a manger for the firm's compliance in accordance with the SRA regime), and any other managers or supervisors who need to be aware.

What Happens If I Find a Problem?

All law firms occasionally have compliance issues and problems. I stress all law firms as humans make mistakes, and even when I was a sole practitioner with my knowledge, occasionally, silly things would occur such as omitting a client care letter prior to commencing the work due to urgency or workload. The purpose of audits is to ensure that no systematic failings exist. The most important thing when an issue potentially arises is that it is investigated, assessed, and follow up actions to avoid repetition, and to avoid an ongoing risk are taken to both manage the situation, and to mitigate the enforcement risk from an SRA perspective.

If the potential breach is "material" under the SRA COLP and COFA regime, then, of course, it must be reported without delay. A material breach is defined by the SRA rather vaguely, and if in doubt, a report to the SRA should be made immediately. If deciding a breach is not material, then record your reasoning contemporaneously and retain that record of your thinking in case the SRA ever ask to see it.

Practical Tips

- Focus on the evidence and follow the evidence and the money in any relationship between a law firm and a CMC;
- Develop a system to audit your particular CMC offering. Focus on the guidance in the other chapters as to where the most risks are likely, dependant upon the type of CMC you have engaged;
- Ensure that the COLP and COFA and Authorised Managers have regular reports (at least monthly) if they are not undertaking these tasks themselves.

Conclusion

The audit position is something which is essential but is a time focused resource. I strongly recommend creating your own Excel spreadsheet to log daily issues so that you can assess any patterns and minimise the time that needs to be spent on a task such as this to enhance the likelihood of it being effective. The audit function, whilst a relatively short chapter in this book, is in fact the shield from SRA enforcement action for most law firms. Make use of the checklists at the back of this book, but also create and develop your own further checklists bespoke to your firm and its risks. If you are not sure, get external support and advice.

CHAPTER ELEVEN
WHAT ABOUT CONFIDENTIALITY?

Introduction

When a law firm works in conjunction with any third parties, there is a risk that confidential information is shared with third parties by either the CMC, or the law firm, without clients providing express consent to such information sharing.

The greater the complexity of the firm and the CMCs relationship and the closer they work together then the more heightened is the risk to confidentiality that is arising.

On 9 January 2015, the SRA published ethics guidance entitled "Protecting and Maintaining Client Confidentiality". This referred to the fact that there are a number of pressures facing law firms, and sets out when they should put the pressures to one side to focus on their regulatory obligations.

It is worth bearing in mind at all times that guidance from regulators can change and the Courts can reinterpret legislation and professional obligations at any time. Nothing is certain in this field. Additionally, this book is not legal advice. My publisher wants me to remind you in each Chapter that you should instruct me to give advice on your specific situation if you need it. The factual circumstances your business faces can be assessed and advised on in context which a book simply cannot do.

Fundamental Starting Point

You must keep the affairs of your client confidential unless disclosure is required or permitted by law, or the client gives informed consent (this is to meet Outcome 4.1).

As the SRA's guidance note from 9 January 2015 states:

"The client should have been given an opportunity to object to disclosure, rather than consent being assumed."

Why Are You Sharing the Information?

If you are sharing information with a third party, including a CMC, ask yourself why you are doing so. The reasons for sharing types of information between, for example, a CMC and a law firm, should be recorded. Consent for that sharing should be obtained expressly in the Client Care Letter, for example, by noting as follows:

"Your matter was introduced to this firm by ABC Limited, a Claims Management Company regulated by the Claims Management Regulator. As part of our commercial relationship with them, we will confirm that we have taken on your matter and we will pay them the fee which comes from our resources, and does not affect the amount of damages you may receive. We need your permission to do this. By returning this document to us signed, and agreeing to our terms and conditions of business, you are agreeing that we may share the fact that we are acting for you with the CMC. We will not share the details of your claim, or any personal information, including, for example, medical information, without your express permission."

Information to the clients should set out, explicitly, the circumstances when and to whom information will be made available, why they need access to the information, and why the disclosure is necessary.

Confidentiality and Legal Professional Privilege

If you share information that is confidential with third parties, you risk, not only being in breach of Chapter 4 of the Code of Conduct 2011 without the client's consent or a legal reason to do so, but you risk waiving legal professional privilege which protects the confidential powers of clients, and once waived by a law firm, can give rise to other third parties being able to access the same information. If, for example, you are instructing an expert witness, there will be important safeguards in place regarding the status of this information, and what can be shared with the Court or Tribunal. This contrasts with the same information being shared with a CMC which could waive legal professional privilege and could give rise to having to disclose other materials to other parties, including the defendants.

When developing a policy of what you must share with your CMCs to make your commercial relationship work, you should, therefore, record what steps you are taking to protect both confidential information, and information which is legally privileged. This should form part of your Risk Register with your COLP verifying how you are managing that risk on a periodic basis through your Risk Register.

Practical Tips

1. Does legal professional privilege apply? If it does apply, does the client need to consent to waiving legal privilege or does legal privilege operate to protect the material i.e. as part of litigation privilege?

2. Has your client consented to the sharing of information with your CMC? If the answer is no, then the client's information should not be shared with that CMC or any third parties.

3. What evidence of consent to share data do you need to ensure you can demonstrate to the SRA and ICO your compliance with your obligations?

Asking these questions is an essential prerequisite towards compliance.

Conclusion

The challenge of confidentiality is to put the client's interests above that of the firm's and its commercial partners, including the CMCs. You should evidence that this is always the case. If you are in any doubt as to whether or not it is appropriate to disclose information, or whether or not the client is giving informed consent (whether because of their vulnerability or their failure to return a document), you should presume that consent has not yet been given or is not informed and maintain confidentiality.

CHAPTER TWELVE
CONCLUSION

It is worth bearing in mind at all times that guidance from regulators can change and the Courts can reinterpret legislation and professional obligations at any time. Nothing is certain in this field. Additionally, this book is not legal advice. My publisher wants me to remind you in each Chapter that you should instruct me to give advice on your specific situation if you need it. The factual circumstances your business faces can be assessed and advised on in context which a book simply cannot do.

Working with CMCs for personal injury law firms is not a simple sign-up and forget about it commercial relationship. As each of the chapters of this book have set out, there are different challenges at different stages of the commercial relationship, but also as part of the client journey from accident to compensation.

Since the SRA was separated from the Law Society, the emphasis has increasingly been on demonstrating compliance through evidence and record keeping and systems and processes. If you want to work with CMCs as a law firm, it is vital that you accept and embrace the challenge to evidence each and every aspect of that relationship.

Doing so enables you to use commercial partners and to place some of the compliance burden on those commercial partners to supply information and to demonstrate their own compliance to you upon audit so that you, as a firm, share that burden with them thus making the relationship commercially viable.

Firms who want to sign an agreement, pay for cases and forget about the relationship will never be able to demonstrate their compliance to the SRA, the ICO or, in the case of the CMC themselves, to the CMR upon audit. The presumption must always be, in the enhanced regulatory environment in which we now practise, that you will be called upon to evidence the matters discussed in this book. The checklists in the following section are designed to help you. You will need to tailor them, however, to your business, and you will need to tailor the timescales for repeating actions to your business. Each of these chapters is designed to be self-contained to give you an overview of the challenges in that particular sphere, this reflects that not all firms will market work in all ways, and some CMCs will only operate one type of marketing, whereas others will operate all types of marketing and different auditing and due diligence requirements will exist. Embrace the challenge, and you could be one of the survivors. Ignore the challenge, and you will be burdened in the event of an investigation. Personal injury is one of the most challenging areas of practice within the legal profession. It is certainly, as was set out in the introduction to this book, one of the most heavily regulated. Knowing that it is so heavily regulated justifies the time spent to read this book and to follow the processes and systems recommended therein. Good luck in meeting the challenges ahead, and enjoy finding out about the businesses you work in conjunction with, and how they demonstrate their compliance and their focus on putting the client first.

CHAPTER THIRTEEN
CHECKLISTS

These two checklists are a good starting point to help you apply the learning and information from the earlier Chapters to your business.

By their nature they are generic and designed to cover common issues. They should help you identify when you need to do more due diligence and more checks on your law firm's suppliers.

They are not of course specific advice and they cannot be relied on as legal advice so should be considered a starting point to apply your own judgement to. If you need legal advice you should commission it and if you are not sure if you do or not then assume that you do.

It is worth bearing in mind at all times that guidance from regulators can change and the Courts can reinterpret legislation and professional obligations at any time. Nothing is certain in this field. Additionally, this book is not legal advice. My publisher wants me to remind you in each Chapter that you should instruct me to give advice on your specific situation if you need it. The factual circumstances your business faces can be assessed and advised on in context which a book simply cannot do.

CHECKLIST A FOR MONITORING A LAW FIRM'S CMC RELATIONSHIPS

See: Code of Conduct (2011) Chapter 8 (Publicity): "IB (8.6) Allowing any other person to conduct publicity for your firm or in-house practice in a way that would breach the principles".

You as a law firm and individual solicitor/regulated person are responsible for what is done which promotes your firm – therefore challenge, assess and evidence compliance at all stages.

Does the telemarketing campaign:

- ☐ Clearly identify the CMCs business name?
- ☐ Provide valid calling-line identification?
- ☐ Ensure that the telesales staff provide the relevant company details on request?
- ☐ Use telesales staff that have the necessary training and competence?
- ☐ Ensure that no high pressure selling is used?
- ☐ Make explicit to clients their right to seek further advice and shop around?
- ☐ Make reasonable enquiries into whether the client has alternative mechanism for making a claim?
- ☐ Use an automated marketing message only with prior consent to contact potential clients?

- □ Have a process for identifying and dealing with vulnerable consumers?
- □ Have a due diligence and monitoring process for outsourced or third party activity?
- □ Have consent to contact potential consumers on the TPS register?
- □ Screen third party data against the TPS register?
- □ Have a "do not call" request and suppression process?

Does the CMCs email marketing campaign:

- □ Use opted in data?
- □ Can the CMC produce the opt in pack of 10% clients randomly selected by you each month?
- □ Have no false, misleading or exaggerated statements?
- □ Have the correct use of "no win no fee" (as per the CAP Code)?

Does the CMCs website have:

- □ Their full legal entity name (as it appears on their MOJ certificate)?
- □ Their trading names. Have they declared their trading names to the Claims Management Regulator?

- ☐ Their geographical address (a PO Box address only is insufficient)?
- ☐ Their contact email address?
- ☐ The regulatory statement "ABC is regulated by the Claims Management Regulator in respect of regulated claims management activities. Its registration is recorded on the website www.justice.gov.uk/claims-regulation" (they must not use the MOJ logo or Royal Coat of Arms where referring to their authorisation)?
- ☐ Their limited company registration details (registered office address, registration number and country of registration)?

Does the CMC display the correct details for the Claims Management Regulator:

Address:
57 – 60 High Street, Burton-upon-Trent, Staffordshire, DE14 1JS

Email: consumer@claimsregulation.gov.uk

THESE CHECKS SHOULD BE CARRIED OUT PRIOR TO COMMENCEMENT OF THE RELATIONSHIP, AFTER ONE MONTH AND THEN QUARTERLY.

CHECKLIST B
DATABASE SUPPLIER
DUE DILIGENCE PROCEDURE

It is worth bearing in mind at all times that guidance from regulators can change and the Courts can reinterpret legislation and professional obligations at any time. Nothing is certain in this field. Additionally, this book is not legal advice. My publisher wants me to remind you in each Chapter that you should instruct me to give advice on your specific situation if you need it. The factual circumstances your business faces can be assessed and advised on in context which a book simply cannot do.

1. **Why do this?**

1.1. To show you conduct your business in an ethical secure manner. Evidence your firm is acting professionally, fairly and with integrity in all its marketing, business dealings and relationships.

2. **Purpose of Procedure**

2.1. The purpose of this procedure is to:

a) set out our responsibilities, and of those working for us, in conducting due diligence checks on our Data Suppliers;

b) ensure that the relevant consent has been obtained from the consumer to be contacted by us for the purposes of our marketing campaign(s);

c) provide information and guidance to those working for us on how to conduct due diligence of Data Suppliers and recognise and deal with any due diligence / consent issues.

2.2. This procedure is intended to be a checklist to assist with establishing consent and compliance. When completing ANNEXES

A, B, C and D, the following guidance, copies of which are available from the Director, should be referred to:-

a) Conduct of Authorised Persons Rules 2014;

b) Marketing and Advertising Guidance for Claims Management Companies; and

c) Information Commissioner's Office Guidance on Direct Marketing.

3. **Who must comply with this policy?**

3.1. This policy applies to all persons working for us or on our behalf in any capacity, including employees at all levels, directors, officers, agency workers, seconded workers, volunteers, interns, agents, contractors, external consultants, third-party representatives and business partners, sponsors, or any other person associated with us, wherever located.

4. **Who is responsible for the policy?**

4.1. [INSERT NAME] (the "Director") has overall responsibility for ensuring this procedure complies with the applicable regulations, and that all those under our control comply with it.

4.2. The Director is responsible for implementing this procedure, monitoring its use and effectiveness, dealing with any queries about it, and auditing internal control systems and procedures to ensure that this due diligence procedure is effective and evidence of consent from consumers for us to contact them is being obtained by Data Suppliers.

4.3. If you have any comments on this procedure or wish to suggest ways in which it might be improved. Comments, suggestions and queries should be addressed to the Director.

5. **Due Diligence Procedure**

5.1. At the outset and prior to any data being purchased from the Data Supplier or used by us, the relevant documents at ANNEX A must be obtained and retained on file.

5.2. If the relevant documents cannot be obtained or it appears that the Data Supplier is not compliant and/or not obtaining the necessary consent, then the data must not be purchased or used.

5.3. Once data has been checked and purchased from the data supplier, further checks should be made periodically every 28 days (ANNEX B), 6 months (ANNEX C) and 12 months (ANNEX D).

5.4. If at any point it appears that the Data Supplier is not compliant and/or obtaining the necessary consent, then the marketing campaign using that data must cease immediately.

ANNEX A
COMPLETE THIS CHECKLIST PRIOR TO BUYING OR USING ANY DATA

Name of person completing Annex A:

Name of proposed Data Supplier:

Date checklist completed:

DOCUMENTS	YES	NO	COMMENTS
Data Supplier checks:			
Companies House • Does the company number match the company name? • Does the registered address match the trading address (If not, why not)? Directors • Who are they? • Do they appear online as reputable? Shareholders • Who are they? • Do they appear online as reputable?			

Have we collected proof of the Data Supplier's registration with the CMR (if relevant)?	
Have we collected proof of Data Supplier's registration with the ICO?	
Have we done an internet search of the Data Supplier's name for adverse comments?	
Obtain copies of staff training records (if relevant).	
Have we obtained a data card on the lists we are considering buying or renting? Ensure the data contains the following information: • When the data was last updated? • Whether the list has been cleaned against the TPS and our own suppression list? • How the data has been collected? • How the data can be used?	

Consent checks:	
If required to do so by the SRA can we show: a) How consent was obtained? b) Who obtained it? c) That the consent was for personal injury claims marketing purposes expressly? d) When was the consent obtained? e) What was the customer told by the organisation recording their consent?	
Does the Data Supplier update their suppression list every 28 days?	
Do they exclude TPS Service customers at point of supply?	
Clarification of options to receive marketing: a) Are the opt-ins clear? b) Is the opt-in for personal injury/ the purpose of our marketing?	

c) Have we reviewed all websites and places where data will be/has been collected and are we satisfied they are not misleading (have we recorded an electronic version of this so we can show a regulator if required)?
Check sign-up process • Have we gone through the process ourselves to check that it is clear to our customers what they are signing up for? Who did this? What records are kept? • Check that the customer is not being forced into receiving marketing communications.
If the Data Supplier obtains customer data via <u>TELESALES</u>, the following should be obtained and completed:
Copy of Data Supplier's marketing/survey script (if relevant)
Copy of Data Supplier's auto-dialler statistics (if relevant)

• Do they comply with Direct Marketing Association (DMA) requirements? • Do they comply with Ofcom requirements? • What evidence of this can the Company supply to our own regulators pre-purchase and with each data set purchased?
Copy of any automated messages (if relevant) • Do they provide their identity? • Do they provide their contact address and Freephone number?
If the Data Supplier obtains customer data via <u>SMS MARKETING</u>, the following should be obtained and completed:
Copy of SMS messages used
Does the SMS message include details of where the recipient can obtain the full company details?
Does the Data Supplier ensure that the SMS message: • Is legal, decent, honest and truthful?

• Is obviously identifiable as a telemarketing communication? • Does not imply the expressions of opinion or subjective claims?
If the Data Supplier obtains customer data via <u>EMAIL MARKETING</u>, the following should be obtained and completed:
Copy of email message
If the Data Supplier obtains customer data via <u>WEBSITE MARKETING</u>, the following should be obtained and completed:
Check the Data Supplier's website (and obtain screen shots) for the following: • the name of the Data Supplier's business (if the business is a limited company it should provide the full legal entity name, regist • ered office address and registered number and company of registration. If the business is a sole trader business they must provide their name)?

• the geographic address at which the business is established? • the contact details of the business including an electronic address (i.e. email address)?	
If the Data Supplier is authorised by the CMR: • Does their website contain the regulatory statement: "*ABC is regulated by the Claims Management Regulator in respect of Regulated Claims Management activities. Its registration is recorded on website www.justice.gov.uk/claims-regulation*". • Does the Data Supplier's website have details of their complaints handling procedure (does it meet Legal Ombudsman signposting requirements)?	

If the Data Supplier uses TESTIMONIALS, the following should be obtained and completed:	
Can the Data Supplier: • Prove that the testimonials are genuine? • Provide contact details of the person who gave the testimonial? • Provide proof of the persons consent to give the testimonial?	

ANNEX B
COMPLETE THIS CHECKLIST AT LEAST EVERY 28 DAYS

Name of person completing Annex B:

Name of Data Supplier:

Date completed:

DOCUMENT	YES	NO	COMMENTS
EVERY 28 DAYS			
Has the Data Supplier updated its suppression list?			
Does the Data Supplier exclude TPS Service customers at point of supply?			
Have we run our own TPS Screening?			

ANNEX C
COMPLETE THIS CHECKLIST AT LEAST EVERY 6 MONTHS

Name of person completing Annex C:

Name of Data Supplier:

Date completed:

DOCUMENT	YES	NO	COMMENTS
EVERY 6 MONTHS			
Obtain direct proof of the Data Supplier's registration with the CMR (if relevant)?			
Obtain direct proof of the Data Supplier's registration with the ICO?			
Do internet search of the Data Supplier's name for adverse comments?			
Obtain records of consent, including: • How consent was obtained? • Who obtained it? • Is the client for personal injury claims marketing? • When was consent obtained? • What was customer told?			

Clarify opt-ins: • When undertaking any data capture on third-party sites, ensure all opt-ins are clear; • Ask to see all websites and places where data will be/has been collected	
Check sign-up process: • Have we gone through the process ourselves to check that it is clear to our customers what they are signing up for? Who did this? When? What records are held to show this? • How can we check that the customer is not being forced into receiving marketing communications.	
If the Data Supplier obtains customer data via <u>TELESALES</u>, the following should be obtained and completed:	
Copy of Data Supplier's marketing/survey script (if relevant)	

Copy of Data Supplier's auto-dialler statistics (if relevant): • Do they comply with DMA requirements? • Do they comply with Ofcom requirements? • What evidence of this can the Company supply?	
Copy of automated message (if relevant) • Do they provide their identity? • Do they provide their contact address or Freephone number?	
If the Data Supplier obtains customer data via SMS MARKETING, the following should be obtained and completed:	
Copy of SMS messages	
Does the SMS message include details of where the recipient can obtain the full company details?	
Does the Data Supplier ensure that the SMS message: • Is legal, decent, honest and truthful? • Is obviously identifiable as a telemarketing communication?	

• Does not imply the expressions of opinion or subjective claims?
If the Data Supplier obtains customer data via <u>EMAIL MARKETING</u>, the following should be obtained and completed:
Copy of email message
Does the Data Supplier ensure that the email message: • Is legal, decent, honest and truthful? • Identifies the sender; and • Provides a valid address for opt-out requests?

ANNEX D
COMPLETE THIS CHECKLIST AT LEAST EVERY 12 MONTHS

Name of person completing Annex D:

Name of Data Supplier:

Date completed:

DOCUMENT	YES	NO	COMMENTS
EVERY 12 MONTHS			
Companies House • Does the company number match? • Does the registered address match the trading address (If not, why not)? Directors • Who are they? • Do they appear online as reputable? Shareholders • Who are they? • Do they appear online as reputable?			

Obtain copies of staff training records (if relevant).	
Obtain a data card on the lists we are considering buying or renting. Ensure the data contains the following information: • When was the data card last updated? • Whether the list has been cleaned against the TPS and our own suppression list? • How the data has been collected? • How the data can be used?	
If the Data Supplier obtains customer data via <u>WEBSITE MARKETING</u>, the following should be obtained and completed:	
Check the Data Supplier's website (and obtain screen shots) for the following:	

• the name of the Data Supplier's business (if the business is a limited company it should provide the full legal entity name, registered office address and registered number and company of registration. If the business is a sole trader business they must provide their name)? • the geographic address at which the business is established? • the contact details of the business including an electronic address (i.e. email address)?	
If the Data Supplier is authorised by the CMR: • Does their website contain the regulatory statement: "*ABC is regulated by the Claims Management Regulator in respect of Regulated Claims Management activities. Its registration is recorded on website www.justice.gov.uk/claims-regulation*"?	

• Does the Data Supplier's website have details of their complaints handling procedure (does it meet Legal Ombudsman signposting requirements)?
If the Data Supplier uses <u>TESTIMONIALS</u>, the following should be obtained and completed:
Can the Data Supplier: • Prove that the testimonials are genuine? • Provide contact details of the person who gave the testimonial? • Provide proof of the persons consent to give the testimonial?

MORE BOOKS BY LAW BRIEF PUBLISHING

A selection of our other titles available now:

'Ellis and Kevan on Credit Hire, 5th Edition' by Aidan Ellis & Tim Kevan
'RTA Allegations of Fraud in a Post-Jackson Era: The Handbook, 2nd Edition' by Andrew Mckie
'A Practical Guide to Holiday Sickness Claims' by Andrew Mckie & Ian Skeate
'RTA Personal Injury Claims: A Practical Guide Post-Jackson' by Andrew Mckie
'On Experts: CPR35 for Lawyers and Experts' by David Boyle
'An Introduction to Personal Injury Law' by David Boyle
'A Practical Guide to Running Housing Disrepair and Cavity Wall Claims' by Andrew Mckie, Ian Skeate, Simon Redfearn
'A Practical Guide to Claims Arising From Accidents Abroad and Travel Claims' by Andrew Mckie & Ian Skeate
'A Practical Guide to Cosmetic Surgery Claims' by Dr Victoria Handley
'A Practical Guide to Chronic Pain Claims' by Pankaj Madan
'A Practical Guide to Claims Arising from Fatal Accidents' by James Patience
'A Practical Approach to Clinical Negligence Post-Jackson' by Geoffrey Simpson-Scott
'A Practical Guide to Personal Injury Trusts' by Alan Robinson
'Occupiers, Highways and Defective Premises Claims: A Practical Guide Post-Jackson' by Andrew Mckie
'Employers' Liability Claims: A Practical Guide Post-Jackson' by Andrew Mckie
'A Practical Guide to Subtle Brain Injury Claims' by Pankaj Madan

'The Law of Driverless Cars: An Introduction' by Alex Glassbrook
'A Practical Guide to Costs in Personal Injury Cases' by Matthew Hoe
'A Practical Guide to Alternative Dispute Resolution in Personal Injury Claims – Getting the Most Out of ADR Post-Jackson' by Peter Causton, Nichola Evans, James Arrowsmith
'A Practical Guide to Personal Injuries in Sport' by Adam Walker & Patricia Leonard
'A Practical Guide to Marketing for Lawyers' by Catherine Bailey & Jennet Ingram
'The No Nonsense Solicitors' Practice: A Guide To Running Your Firm' by Bettina Brueggemann
'Baby Steps: A Guide to Maternity Leave and Maternity Pay' by Leah Waller
'The Queen's Counsel Lawyer's Omnibus: 20 Years of Cartoons from the Times 1993-2013' by Alex Steuart Williams

www.ingramcontent.com/pod-product-compliance
Ingram Content Group UK Ltd.
Pitfield, Milton Keynes, MK11 3LW, UK
UKHW020147290926
15471UKWH00004B/732

9 781911 035213